Yorkshire Vol II
Edited by Heather Killingray

CW00515341

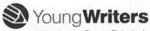 Young**Writers**

First published in Great Britain in 2005 by:
Young Writers
Remus House
Coltsfoot Drive
Peterborough
PE2 9JX
Telephone: 01733 890066
Website: www.youngwriters.co.uk

All Rights Reserved

© Copyright Contributors 2005

SB ISBN 1 84602 223 1

Foreword

Young Writers was established in 1991 and has been passionately devoted to the promotion of reading and writing in children and young adults ever since. The quest continues today. Young Writers remains as committed to the fostering of burgeoning poetic and literary talent as ever.

This year's Young Writers competition has proven as vibrant and dynamic as ever and we are delighted to present a showcase of the best poetry from across the UK. Each poem has been carefully selected from a wealth of *Playground Poets* entries before ultimately being published in this, our thirteenth primary school poetry series.

Once again, we have been supremely impressed by the overall high quality of the entries we have received. The imagination, energy and creativity which has gone into each young writer's entry made choosing the best poems a challenging and often difficult but ultimately hugely rewarding task - the general high standard of the work submitted amply vindicating this opportunity to bring their poetry to a larger appreciative audience.

We sincerely hope you are pleased with our final selection and that you will enjoy *Playground Poets Yorkshire Vol II* for many years to come.

Contents

Aberford CE Primary School

Raif Fletcher (10)   1
Sarah Pedley (10)   1
Gabrielle Kirby (10)   2
Emily Land (10)   2
Jorja McClay (11)   3
Lottie Akers-Dunphy (11)   3
Emma-Jane Hills (11)   4
Danielle Smith (10)   4
Lauren Hardcastle (9)   5

Ashdell Preparatory School

Frances Brailsford (9)   5
Rebecca Bridge (10)   6
Charley Barker (9)   6
Verity Bridge (10)   7
Bethany Nutbrown (11)   8
Kate Harben (11)   8
Jenny Utting (11)   9
Megan Blade (10)   10
Rebecca Towning (11)   11
Alexandra Jones (9)   11
Katie Midgley (11)   12
Billie Mills-Pullan (9)   12
Frances Logan (11)   13
Evie Crossland (9)   13
Rhia Walton (10)   14
Hannah Burdall (10)   14
Hannah Poulsom (10)   15
Natasha Bailey (10)   15
Natalie Chan-Lam (9)   16
Natasha Douglas (8)   17
Trishna Kurian (7)   17
Anastasia Paschali (10)   18
Victoria Wensley (9)   18
Chloe Patterson (9)   19
Megan Wolstenholme (10)   19
Lucy Blade (8)   20
Imogen Stables (9)   20

Georgia Blagden (9)   21
Lydia Brooks (9)   21
Imogen Parker (8)   22
Alice Strong (8)   22

Barnby Dun Primary School
Bethany Fletcher (8)   23
Katie Vickers (8)   23
Rachel Grashion (9)   24
Zoe Oxley (8)   25
Ellesha Curry (8)   25
Francis Leanne Fisher (9)   26
Holly Fawley (8)   26

Canon Popham CE Primary School
Natalie Brown (10)   27
Poppy Wickham (9)   27
Megan Sowerby (9)   28
Michael Hattersley (10)   28
Richard Wilkinson (10)   29
Jordan Scholey (10)   29
James Bellamy (10)   30
Rhianna Armstrong (10)   30
Cody Martin (8)   31
Andrew Stratton (10)   31
Lois Nicholson (10)   32
Ruby Bircumshaw (10)   33
Matthew Vann (10)   33
Melissa Tasker (10)   34
Loren Davison (9)   34
Lauren Bruce (9)   35
Alex Woodhouse (9)   35
Holly Bint (9)   36
Christopher Mumford (9)   36

Carlton J&I School
Jody Pringle (11)   37
Brad Allen (11)   37
Todd Bailey (11)   38
Rebecca Watson (10)   38

Damien Zastepa (11)	39
Garth Halford (10)	39
Ashley Bowler (11)	40
Jack Cowell (11)	40
Nathan Kirby (11)	41

Clifton Community Arts School

Harry Baldwin (11)	41
Raechelle Little (12)	42
Tiffany Sterland (11)	42
Harley Blackham (12)	43
Nicole Pimperton (12)	43
Thomas Watts (12)	43
Emily Passmore-Bailey (11)	44
Amy Blacow (12)	44
Abir Hussain (12)	44
Nathan Duckmanton (12)	45
Sophie Davis (12)	45
Jordan Tracey (11)	45
Tanya Gooding (12)	45
Kara Sanders (12)	46
Kesley Hickman (12)	46
Reece Eblet (11)	46
Sally Morton (12)	46
Sydhra Bi (12)	47
Uzma Parveen (11)	47
Chantelle Woodthorpe (12)	47

Drighlington Primary School

Aimee Inskip (8)	48
Charlotte Mills (9)	48
Sarah Kelley (10)	49
Jack Bentley (9)	49
Lauren Eastwood (10)	50
Thomas Gilpin (9)	50
Lauren Newsome (10)	51
Keely Runton (8)	51
Geena Gaskell (10)	52
Louise Raper (10)	52
Chanice Mallett (10)	53
Jadean Mosley (8)	53

Samantha Ingles (10)   54
Hetty Sunderland (10)   54
Alice Pearson (10)   55
Jay Milomo (7)   55
Timothy Shotbolt (10)   56
Charlotte Lyles (10)   56
Ashleigh Henry (10)   57
Oliver Moody (10)   57
Harriet Hanson (10)   58
Gabbi Pashley (10)   59
Adam Tyas (10)   59
George Booth (8)   60
Elsie Smith (10)   60
Olivia Jones (10)   61
Bradley O'Donnell (8)   61
Adam Stocks (10)   62
Daniel Roberts (8)   62
Emma Edwards (8)   63
Luke Simpson (8)   63
Harry Lupton (7)   63
Jordan Hobbah (9)   64
George Lewis (10)   64
Reece Farnhill (9)   65
Sam Lupton (10)   65
Oliver Sullivan (10)   65
Shelbi Hoole (9)   66
Alex Gidley (9)   66
Charlotte Thompson (9)   67
Harry Ferguson (9)   67
Luke Sugden (8)   68
Christopher Goult (9)   68
Alex Lewis (8)   69
Thomas Farrar (9)   69
Jacob Rodgers (8)   70
Ben Bridge (9)   70
James Harrison (9)   71
Jasmine Gray (8)   71
Harvey Dibb (8)   72
Adam Banwell (8)   72
Jake Holt (9)   73
Katie Elsom (9)   73
Elliot Beasley (9)   74

Kelsey McDonald (9)	74
Kelly Wilkinson (9)	74
Jade Hustler (8)	75
Jennifer Cable (9)	75
Mac Taylor (9)	75
Lauren Taylor (9)	76
Jordan Stretton (9)	76
Adam Stevens (9)	76
Cain Harniess (9)	77
Lucy Solomons (8)	77
Liam Bailey (9)	77
George Bentley (7)	78
Reece Matthews (8)	78
Ben Mitchell (8)	79
Calum Hepworth (9)	79
Jennifer Davies (9)	80
Andrew Bailey (9)	80
Amelia Grey (9)	80
Gregory Barker (9)	81
Luke Austin (9)	81
Robbie Gaskell (7)	82
Oliver Wilkinson (8)	82
Ellie Carney (8)	83
Sam Hanson (8)	83
Brandon Byrne (8)	84
Declan Smith (8)	84
Georgina Holmes (8)	85
Jack Day (7)	85
Sasha Beardsley & Bethany Clark (10)	86
Callum Hargraves & Jack Bradford (10)	86
Bradley Pickles & Abigail Housecroft (9)	87
Kieran Boulton (8)	87
Jack Wilson (10)	88
Marc Willis (8)	88
Robert Jones (10)	89
Jake Carney (8)	89
Michael Smithson (9)	90
Jordan Sullivan (7)	90
Grace Daji (9)	91
Benn Sharp (7)	91
Jodie Mitchell (9)	92
Chris Hanson (9)	92

Sarah Cowles (8)   93
Timothy Tomlinson (8)   93
Libby Wilson (7)   93
Keely Cooper (8)   94
George Williamson (8)   94
Lila Kara-Zaitri (8)   94
Jobe Rennard (7)   95
Jack Walker (8)   95
Abigail Waller (8)   95

Hawksworth CE Primary School
Simon Lovitt (8)   96
Ella Lefley (8)   96
Garth Darwin (8)   96
Amy Turk (9)   97
Daniel Holt (9)   97
Elizabeth Heard (9)   97
Lizzie Ayre (8)   98
Sam Chilvers (8)   98
Joseph Mountain (8)   99
Cameron Scott (8)   99
Rhys Austwick-Holland (8)   99
Amy Swales (8)   100
Isabel Simmen (8)   100
Mitchell Wellman-Brown (8)   100
William McLaughlin (8)   101
Ella Sagar (8)   101
Francesca Smith (8)   101

Inglebrook School
Ashleigh Brain (11)   102
Rachel Connell (11)   102
Ellis Birkby (11)   103
Thomas Copley (11)   103
Parice Fenning (10)   104
Francesca Payne (9)   105
Ben Newman (10)   106
Kate Lovatt (10)   107
Megan Stephens (9)   108
Georgina Freeman (9)   109
Karan Pugal (10)   110

Charlotte Barker (10)   110
Rowena Jenkins (10)   111
Luke Whitaker (10)   111
Leah Bygrave (10)   112
Nick Howarth (10)   112

Manston St James Primary School
Isobel Leaverland (8)   113

Park Road Primary School
Luke Hemming (10)   113
Joshua McCann (9)   114
Zainab Hafejee (10)   114
Bilaal Valla (9)   115
James Aston (10)   115
Sarrah Ammar (10)   116
Lauren North (8)   116
Ashia Zaneb (9)   117
Huzaifa Motara (9)   117
Lucy Hodgson (9)   118
Atif Farid (9)   118
Shazaib Hussain (9)   119
Rabeeah Ammar (9)   119
Nadia Asif (9)   120
Mohammad Tayyab Ashraf (9)   120
Talha Daji (9)   121
Hamzah Islam (9)   121
Jack Robinson (9)   122
Kieran Bennett (9)   122
Iqra Amjad (9)   123
Chloe Hammill (8)   123
Safina Bi (9)   124

St Joseph's RC Primary School, Castleford
Gabrielle Renavent (9)   124
Evan Lynch (10)   125
Jordan Cairns (11)   125
Louise Farr (10)   126
Fiona Appleton (11)   126
Hannah McGrath (10)   127

Mark Newson (9)   127
Jordan Fort (11)   128
Liam Beck (10)   128
Jack Farr (11)   128
John Adey (10)   129
Bethany Jones (11)   129
Rachel Gray (11)   129
Connor Mulvaney-Walls (11)   130
Bethany Goodson (11)   130
Katie Smith (10)   130
Natalie Tracey (11)   131
Joshua Gallagher (11)   131
Amy Howley (11)   131
Grace Brookman (11)   132
Edward Maskill (11)   132
Kirsty Newman (11)   132
Nathaniel Greening (10)   133
Reef Bray (10)   133
Jessica Sharpe (11)   133
Amy Rumney (10)   134

St Joseph's RC Primary School, Wetherby
Christian Walton (11)   134
Emily Legg (11)   135
Maeve Anderson (10)   135
Sophie Crayford (11)   136
Adam Waterfield (11)   137
Rachel Keighley (11)   137

St Margaret's CE Primary School, Leeds
Rosie Baker (11)   138
Emily Hall (11)   139
Emma Jeffries (11)   139
Elizabeth Roughton (11)   140
Rebecca Daw (10)   140
Sarah Roughton (11)   141
Rachel Akhondi (10)   141
Hannah Walton (10)   142
Freya A Chappell (10)   142
Molly Pickering (9)   143
Helen Wilson (11)   143

Sophie Baker (9)   144
Jacob Brown (10)   145
Daniel Ramsden (9)   145
Lizzie Lloyd (9)   146
Amber Tallentire (10)   146
Kate Blackburn (10)   147
Christopher Caress (10)   147
Alexander Sherriff (10)   148
Charlotte Marsden (10)   148
Lois Davies (10)   149
Kiera Verity (10)   149
Darius Baghban (10)   150
Emma Lumb (9)   150
Alexander Wood (10)   151
Wayne Sandham (10)   151
Lois Brown (11)   152
Jessica Womack (10)   153
Kieran Olsen (10)   153
Nathaniel Warnes (10)   154
Toni-Louise Stanley (10)   154
Joshua Malone (9)   155
Aimee McKellar (10)   155
Thomas Harris (10)   156
Pollyanna Yeadon (10)   156
Andrew Edser (10)   157
Rosie Woodgate (10)   157
Dominic Fogden (10)   158

St Matthias' CE Primary School, Leeds
Jade Corbridge (10)   158
Misbah Zahir (9)   159
Emma Terrell (10)   159
Eamon Droko (10)   160
Reece George (9)   160

St Thomas More RC Primary School, Sheffield
Shannon Wharton (9)   161
Alex Barker (11)   161
Chloe Ingram (9)   162
Ruby Doane (9)   163
Kimberley Revill (9)   164

William Hodkin (9)   164
Bronia Johnston (8)   165
William Matthews (9)   166
Rebecca Monfredi (9)   166
Matthew Carter (10)   167
Ethan Barton (9)   167
Chloe Start (10)   168
Michaela Revill (11)   169
Eleanor Gott (10)   170
Emma Townsend (11)   171
Ella Jeffcock (10)   172
Russell Marsden (10)   173
Thomas Needham (9)   174
Malcolm Smith (11)   175
Rachael Bradley (10)   176
Thomas Smith (9)   176
Catherine Monfredi (9)   177
Caitlin Ryan (8)   177
Bradley Phillips (9)   178
Karis Dykes (9)   178
Rebecca Bradley (10)   179
Esme Hazelby (10)   179

Snaith CP School

Jade Evans (10)   180
Harry Agar (11)   180
Josh Breeden (9)   181
Jack Taylor (9)   182
Holly Price (9)   183
Chloe Smith (10)   183
Charley Britton (9)   184
Elizabeth Holroyd (11)   184
Kevin Moles (10)   185
James McKiernan (9)   185
Sarah Dick (9)   186
Molly Roper (10)   187
Georgia Thompson (9)   187
Katie Oliver (11)   188
Gabi Wright (9)   188
Joe Ford (9)   189
Robyn Bligh (9)   189

Lewis Kellett (10)	190
Aaron Oxley (10)	190
Amy Oglesby (10)	191
Evie Childs (10)	191
Stephanie Wigg (9)	192
Naomi Sweetman (9)	192
Izzy Procter (8)	193
Sophia Christou (9)	193
Steven Fearnley (10)	194
Madeline Gallagher (8)	194
Heather King (11)	195
Katy Sharp (9)	195
Rebecca Knowles (11)	196
Thomas Boddye (9)	196
Evie Whiteley (8)	197
Georgia Kees (9)	197
Ryan Cotterill (8)	198
Molly Thompson (9)	198
Kristina Curtis (8)	199
Aidan Kirsopp (8)	199
Macauley Thornton (8)	200
Jonathan Crossley (11)	200
Rose Thornton (8)	201
Charlotte Dudley (7)	201
Jack Wilson (8)	202
Callum Chapman (7)	202
Jake Howard (7)	203
Michael King (7)	203
Ben Roper (8)	204
Harry Walton (7)	204
Jodie Gilson (7)	205
Megan Backhouse (7)	205
Luke Wilson (7)	206
Georgie Smith (8)	206
Rachel Tate (7)	207
Bethany Knight (7)	207
Sean Younger (7)	208
Holly Denby (7)	208

Walkeringham Primary School

Amy Mackenzie (8)	209
Iona Murray (9)	209
Jack Rogers (11)	210
Emma Frost (10)	210
Zach Beard (9)	211
Megan Pearcy (8)	211
Jake Beard (11)	212
Beth Burley (10)	212
Jack Bramham (11)	213
Katie-Ann Wickens (9)	213
Aaron Green (8)	214
Nick Rodgers (11)	214
Rebecca Langley (9)	215

Wakefield Girls' High School Junior School

Bhagyashree Ganguly (9)	215
Hannah Slack (8)	216
Samantha Lancaster (9)	217
Lorna Bowers (9)	217
India Copley (9)	218
Katie Idle (8)	219
Louise Belton (9)	219
Olivia McGrath (9)	220
Hannah Foy (9)	220
Rebecca Morris (9)	221
Rebecca Hick (9)	221
Rosie Allsopp (9)	222
Elizabeth Ward (9)	222
Mary Tadross (9)	223
Rachel Sugarman (9)	223
Alexandra Selby (9)	223

Westways Primary School

Jack Hanlon (11)	224
Cara Bradshaw-King (9)	225
Adday Heller (9)	226
Amy Taylor (11)	226
Holly Bowman (11)	227
Jack Bowman (5)	227

Tom Bowman (7)   228
Meg Plowright (9)   228
Sanaa Ghori (10)   229
Joanna Lee (9)   229
Denver Baxter (11)   230
Jessie Dooley (9)   230
Michael Wilsher (11)   231
Sam Tadhunter (9)   231
Ceara Stones (11)   232
Beth Fairhurst (9)   232
Antonia Dore (9)   233
Claire Wilsher (9)   234

The Poems

Rugby

Rugby is a game to play
So I shall play it everyday.
Rough and tumble,
Tackle and fall
I will always play the ball.
We pass it along
Away it flies
We can score
A lot of tries.
We line it up
To take the kick?
Take your pick.
As the final whistle blows
We all shout, 'Yes'
As we have won.

Raif Fletcher (10)
Aberford CE Primary School

My Cat

She is waiting for me
Eyes glowing
Waiting patiently for food
As I walk into the house
Following me around
I even go into the room
She follows me there
I sit on the couch
She sits on my knee
And I realise that my
Little pussycat is safe with me.

Sarah Pedley (10)
Aberford CE Primary School

Summer

The summer sun shines brightly,
As lambs frolic in the field,
The clouds dance and scatter around,
While birds sing their graceful tune.
Flowers bloom and bees buzz,
Deer drink out of the trickling stream,
And all along the badgers dream,
Of night-time wonders and wiggly worms.
Now the sun sets, all is quiet,
Not a flicker in the field,
But now and then we hear a tune,
No buzzing bees, just the trickling stream,
It's always kept secret,
Summer.

Gabrielle Kirby (10)
Aberford CE Primary School

Waiting

Cat's eyes scintillate
Burning in the black of dark
Waiting for a single movement
Ready to pounce.

Cat and mouse frozen in time,
Each waiting for the other,
Mouse eyes filled with fear
Cat's with a greedy hunger.

Emily Land (10)
Aberford CE Primary School

Fallen Angels

Once I saw an angel
Disguised as a stallion horse,
Galloping across the dark canvas
Of the night's sky.
Its snowy-white mane flowing
Through the cool air,
And its silk feather wings
Rustling gently through the breeze.

Then I saw another angel
Falling from the sky,
I looked up to Heaven
And there I saw a smile,
A smile I recognised
From a picture I had kept,
A picture of my grandad
The one I never met.

Jorja McClay (11)
Aberford CE Primary School

The World Within My Mind

My imagination free as a dream,
My dreams to bring me hope,
Hope to set determination,
My spirit to take me where I dare go,
These words come from my mind,
Which is full of words unsaid,
A mystical world of hope and dreams,
Deep inside my head.

Lottie Akers-Dunphy (11)
Aberford CE Primary School

Water

Imagine the gentle water trickling
Through your toes.

The wet, the coldness,
The changing colours.

Gliding past whilst
Sitting, watching, waiting,
Waiting for a different shape to appear.

Looking out across the still water
Shining, shimmering in the sunlight
Like a diamond jewel.

Here the waves splash on the rocks
Until they die
Away, away, away . . .

Emma-Jane Hills (11)
Aberford CE Primary School

My New Footie Boots

My new footie boots are great
Leather tough as rhino skin
With studs as hard as granite
And the colour black as night.

These boots of mine are full of goals
And tackles not yet made.

If I scored four goals in all
These golden boots would be the best
Providing magic on the ball.

Danielle Smith (10)
Aberford CE Primary School

Who Am I?

Its legs go forwards and backwards
As it trots around the field,
The smell of hay and carrots
The feeling of being free.

Its eyes sparkle and shine
Like diamonds in the sun
Feel the knots as you brush its mane
Put the saddle on and get ready to go.

Up and down the grassy hills
A whispering breeze from the wind
Faster then slower every stop
Calm down after a busy day
Go in the field and play.

Lauren Hardcastle (9)
Aberford CE Primary School

My Dad

He's a bright red Ferrari zooming down the road.
He's like a monkey playing tricks,
A sparkly dragon, gilted in gold.
He's like a football bouncing along the street,
He's like hot summer sunshine at midday.
He feels like a soft, cuddly teddy bear,
He sounds like a deep blue ocean.

Frances Brailsford (9)
Ashdell Preparatory School

The Hunt

The horn sounded as countless men on
Horses rushed forwards, their dogs
Scampering between thundering hooves.
Weasels and foxes vacated the meadows
At tremendous speed, while rabbits
Hopped behind, cotton tails bobbing up
And down.
It was these that the huntsmen were after,
bonny brown fur to line cloaks and boots,
red tails tipped with white to make scarves and stoles.
Even the weasels are skinned to make clothes.

A gun was fired, birds evacuated the trees
Turning the sky suddenly black and brown.
Their sleek feathers would go to waste
And their flesh to a tasty pie.
There is a knock on the door.
The men have returned to share the game with us.

Rebecca Bridge (10)
Ashdell Preparatory School

Rebecca D

She's a soft, warm and cuddly puppy,
She's active and as quick as a hare,
She's a colourful pencil case,
The sound of the gazing, salty sea with crashing waves,
She's as silly as a laughing clown doing tricks,
The smell of a pancake with sticky toffee sauce on top,
As tough as a footballer,
She's as fizzy as a glass of pop,
She's a visible door that's always open,
She's bright like the sunshine.

Charley Barker (9)
Ashdell Preparatory School

This Is The Sea

To some people, the sea is a mass of blue ripples,
Cold as ice.
To some people, the sea is a hoard of green seaweed,
Floating about and grabbing at your ankles and wrists.
To some people, the sea is a trove of yellow sand
That feels warm and soft under your feet.
To some people, the sea is a treasury of white,
Dainty shells that shimmer and shine under the water.
To some people, the sea is a school of silver fish
That twist and turn, but never stop.

But to me, the sea is a mass of red danger
That is vivid and clear in my mind.
To me, the sea is a hoard of purple terror that
Strangles and suffocates you.
To me, the sea is a trove of blackness that
Drowns you without mercy.
To me, the sea is a treasury of grey monsters,
That hunt and chase you forever.

The sea is different to everyone and
Everything, just as everyone is different to
Anything and anyone.

Verity Bridge (10)
Ashdell Preparatory School

Stars

Stars are jewels.
They shimmer like glass.
Stars are rays of hope,
Bursting through the sky.
Stars are sweets,
Surprises in wrappers.
Stars are people,
Ones who we know.
Stars are headlights.
They flash before your eyes.
Stars are mobiles,
In a circle above your head.
Stars are pin heads,
Marking signs in the sky.
Stars are you and me;
We are all different,
Yet all the same.

Bethany Nutbrown (11)
Ashdell Preparatory School

The Darkness Of Night

The night is when a mother pulls a
Blanket of stars over her son,
Like a shadow creeping up behind you.
The night sky is a vision of darkness
In which only the stars can be seen.
Stars sparkle through the darkness of night,
Like eyes of a frightened fox.
Street lights shimmer in darkness like
Rays of the sun.
At night the world is at peace.

Kate Harben (11)
Ashdell Preparatory School

My Auntie Hilda (Very Exaggerated)

Her cold hands clasped around me loosely.
Her withered, gnarled fingers tickled my back,
Which was most different to hers.
Hers was bent and twisted like an old willow tree.
Shivers went down my spine at the thought of it.
She lifted her bony body into the chair
And gazed up at me with her small, lonely, slightly critical eyes.
The straight line towards the bottom of her face opened and a croaky
Voice hit my ears. I heard a gentle, calm tint too,
But that was soon covered by a cantankerous tone,
Which drifted towards my brother.
Her nose, twisted and contorted into an unpleasant shape, twitched.
I dared not look at her face any longer.
My gaze, drifting upwards towards the ceiling
Passed through a forest of thin, wispy strands of hair,
Which her head was desperately hanging onto.
At light-speed my eyes dropped downwards,
Away from the ghastly show, to meet an even worse sight.
There her legs lay, dangling from the chair,
Her clear stockings clinging to what was left of her white, spotty skin.
A call came from my mum. It was time to go.
My auntie lifted her heavy bones out of her chair.
The arms came again, but nothing,
No nothing could have prepared me for what came next.
Her face closed in. Her cold lips hit my cheek.
The hairs on her face tickled me, but it was not a tickle of joy,
It was a tickle of doom.
It was a while before I came to my senses again.
When I did, I was in the car, driving away from that awful smell,
A mixture of soaps
And mothballs.
Free at last. Never to be kissed by my auntie Hilda again!

Jenny Utting (11)
Ashdell Preparatory School

Fear

Fear is a dark, powerful hand,
Reaching out of the darkness, surrounding you in peril.
Fear is a man in a black cloak,
A knife glimmering in his hand, hiding in a corner of your room.
Fear is a great demonic animal, with eight huge, hairy legs,
Hiding in the darkness, waiting to pounce.
Fear is a deep, dark whirlpool, sucking you down into
                                            its deadly waters.
Fear is a black hole, lingering in space, plunging the world into
Eternal darkness and death.
Fear is a burning circle of flames, gradually closing in on you.
Fear is a giant thundercloud, always hovering over you,
Constantly reminding you that it is there, with a loud clap.
Fear is a mountain that people climb up, but never climb down.
Fear is a shadow, hiding the actions of thieves and murderers.
Fear is the night sky, a deep, dark hole in the street, a rip
                                            in the world.
Fear is a friend who you thought you could trust,
Who just betrayed you.
Fear is the top of a skyscraper, a deadly drop beneath you.
Fear is a cancer, growing inside you, eating away, destroying you.
Fear is a life changing test, which you are about to sit.
Fear is a huge ocean, which you are swimming in,
Pulling you further and further away from home.
Fear is death, when you have to leave your family,
Friends and life behind you.
Fear is different to everyone and comes in many different forms,
Each more terrifying than the last.

Megan Blade (10)
Ashdell Preparatory School

Night

Through the blanket of darkness, jewels danced merrily across
the sky.
Street lights were a twisting corridor guiding me into the night.
A whistling breeze pushed me forwards, with a high-pitched noise
Following my footsteps.

Shadows pounced towards me, my heart beating like a drum,
But still the wind brutally pushed me into the night.
Bats surrounded me, screeching their sinister call in my ear,
But still, the wind brutally pushed me into the night.
Trees embraced me into their twisting arms,
But still, the wind brutally pushed me into the night.

Two bright eyes, emerging from the carpet of darkness,
approached me.
Suddenly, the wind stopped its piercing cry.
Suddenly, the scheming arms of trees loosened their grip and
slithered away.
The road was silent.
The only thing I could see in the distance were two glistening
Headlights approaching me.

Rebecca Towning (11)
Ashdell Preparatory School

Monsters

Some monsters are huge and hairy,
Some monsters are small and scary,

Some live in caves and some in forests,
Some live in rivers and some in oceans,

Some eat you for breakfast and some for tea,

Some crunch your bones and some suck your blood,

I lie awake at night terrified by the thought . . .
But the one that scares me most is my *mum!*

Alexandra Jones (9)
Ashdell Preparatory School

Night

The day is slowly ending and night is soon to start.
Clouds are gently falling
Like a blanket to tuck us in.
Stars sing a lullaby of hope
As we slowly slumber.

Some animals drift off into a floating dream.
Others start to yawn and wake,
An adventure to begin.

Owls are hunting, their prey prepares to flee.
Lambs seek out their mother.
Foxes wait like a jack-in-the-box, ready to pounce,
Victims unknowingly watched.

The midnight sky is brighter now.
Stars twinkle as darkness reverts to light.
Creatures of the night are homeward bound,
Waiting to steal away into a dream.
Darkness seems to fade as another day is dawning.

Katie Midgley (11)
Ashdell Preparatory School

Nightfall

Golden sun with beaming light,
Falling silently into the dark night,
Dying, to be born again,
Sleeping on its darkened bed,
The light is gone, it is dead.
It splits into the moon and stars,
Till daybreak, when it is resurrected.
Moon and stars will die away,
Mighty sun will beam once more,
Over the misty land,
Over roaring sea and sand.

Billie Mills-Pullan (9)
Ashdell Preparatory School

Fear

Fear is like an everlasting tunnel,
Like a forest that is dark and spooky,
Like an ancient and haunted house.

Fear is like the eternal lump in your throat,
And an injection in a dark, scary room.

A phobia is of spiders, water and fire.
Fear is a feeling which makes you sick inside.
Fear is a feeling which makes you wonder if you
Will live or die.

Fear is like waiting for a result and what it will bring,
Like sitting in the doctor's waiting room,
Waiting, waiting and wondering.

Fear is all of these things and much, much more.
Fear may be thoughts, visions and dreams
But if it becomes real, it's scarier than you could ever imagine.

Frances Logan (11)
Ashdell Preparatory School

Spiders

Eight long hairy legs
Crawling up the wall,
Spiders!
The most terrifying creature of all.

Eight long hairy legs,
Crawl across the floor,
Crawling really fast now,
Towards the bathroom door.

Eight long hairy legs,
Now they are outside.
'Free at last the danger's past,'
The hairy spider cried!

Evie Crossland (9)
Ashdell Preparatory School

People Poem On Hannah Burdall

She's a table that I can always lean on,
Solid and reliable,
A field of red poppies swaying in the cool
Spring breeze,
She's a little cat lying in the hot summer sun,
Content and happy,
The scented smell of a pretty pink rose.
She's a shooting star,
Always full of ideas,
A slice of water melon,
Sweet and fresh.
She's a ray of sunshine,
Brightening up the day,
A small blue rock pool,
Always full of surprises,
A warm evening on a long, sandy beach,
Calm, cool and relaxing.

Rhia Walton (10)
Ashdell Preparatory School

Rhia Walton

She's an extensive, waving palm tree,
A multicoloured door always wide open.
She's a dolphin jumping in the little
Ripples of the sea,
She's a never-ending, white sanded beach.
She's the scent of a lily,
The sound of the waves moving
Backwards and forwards,
A sun setting on the horizon.
A fizzy drink,
A fairy floating in the sky.

Hannah Burdall (10)
Ashdell Preparatory School

The Storm

When the storm winds whistle like howling wolves,
And the pattering of rain grows louder,
When the mountains grow taller in the moonlight,
Then a sudden crash of towering lightning strikes,
And the whispers, crunches and mutters of
The mysterious storm are heard.
But amongst this grey, cold cloud,
A sunray of hope emits through the cold and grey,
As the storm drifts far away for another day.

As the living things come back to light,
Their feet gently pattering on the floor,
A faraway storm is growing,
Crashing, banging and clattering.
Then the old, whispering wind returns,
And the cold chill feel of the rain.
But everything that comes with a start has to end,
As the storm moves on or a bird flies away.

Hannah Poulsom (10)
Ashdell Preparatory School

Four Hoofs

My pet has four hoofs.
He has four legs as well.
His coat is as brown as mud.
His mane a black night.
His voice is louder than a trumpet.
He's as gentle as a fly.
He smells like trees.
He is faster than a bike.
He's my best friend,
And always will be.
He's my *pony*.

Natasha Bailey (10)
Ashdell Preparatory School

Pest At The Seaside

Mum, hurry up, it's time to go
Why are you and Gran always so slow?
We're off to the beach; Mum, Gran and me
To play in the sand, and swim in the sea.

Mum, are we there yet?
You've missed it I bet,
Mum look! There's the sea,
I hear it calling to me.

The water's too cold to have any fun,
And the straps on my swimsuit are coming undone,
Ooh, the sand's tickling my hands,
Mum, you *still* haven't blown up my armbands.

Mum, come here quick!
That boy's giving my sandcastle a kick.
Waah! He's kicked it to the ground,
And all my flags have fallen down.

Mum, I need a towel, I'm all wet,
Can I have an ice cream yet?
Then I want a donkey ride,
But you have to stand right by my side.

What? Time to go already?
But my watch says it's only eleven thirty
What do you mean? I'm not a pest,
You *always* seem to need a rest!

Natalie Chan-Lam (9)
Ashdell Preparatory School

Race Day

I pack my bag
Costume, cap, towels - don't forget the goggles
I'm sure I've remembered, it all, it all, all.

I get to the pool
Butterflies in my tummy
Nervous, nervous, nervous.

My name is called
I prepare to dive
It takes so long, so long, so long.

I hear silence
My arms and legs go round and round
The water is freezing.

It's over
My fingers touch the wall
It's over, over, over.

Prize giving!
My name is called
I've won, won, *won!*

Natasha Douglas (8)
Ashdell Preparatory School

Don't

All people do is say, 'Don't,' why can't they
Ever say anything different?
'Don't throw your socks around.'
'Don't hit your sister.'
'Don't forget to brush your teeth.'
'Don't forget to flush the toilet.'
'Don't throw eggs in your sister's hair.'
'Don't cut your toys' hair.'
'Don't eat too many sweets.'
See what I mean.
Parents can be pure evil.

Trishna Kurian (7)
Ashdell Preparatory School

Aurora

Amazing night
Wonderful night
Stars in the sky
Beaming bright.

I dream of a fairy
With magic wings
She dances around me
And tells me, 'Sweet dreams.'

Her name is Aurora
She sparkles so bright
She kisses and hugs me
And tells me, 'Goodnight.'

Anastasia Paschali (10)
Ashdell Preparatory School

Dolphins

Dolphins, dolphins,
All painted in blue,
As they shimmer and shine,
And dive through and through.

The foamy blue waves,
On the bright sunny day,
It's home for the dolphins,
Who frolic and play.

My friends the dolphins,
Are special to me,
As they swim so sleekly in the deep, blue sea.

Victoria Wensley (9)
Ashdell Preparatory School

The Storm

Thunder roared.
Lightning flashed.
The wind howled as it tore through trees.
As trees crashed to the ground,
A car swivelled and swerved out of the way.

As the storm died away,
The wind turned to a whisper and a gentle breeze.
The neighbourhood lay ruined.
People crept out of their houses like mice.
Standing like statues,
No one could speak,
All was silent,
As they peered at the devastation.

Chloe Patterson (9)
Ashdell Preparatory School

The Storm

Thunder roared.
Lightning split the sky.
Rain beat down.
Trees crashed to the floor.
Wild animals tumbled and twisted,
And scuttled and scattered,
To get away from the blustering storm.

The thunder concluded.
Lightning ended.
Rain faded away.
Trees lay motionless on the ground.
Animals peered and peeped.
The storm had ceased.

Megan Wolstenholme (10)
Ashdell Preparatory School

My Sister

My sister never takes the blame,
Sometimes she can be a pain,
My sister never takes the blame.

My sister doesn't even care,
If sometimes games are not quite fair,
My sister doesn't even care.

My sister normally reads all night,
She totally refuses to turn off the light,
My sister normally reads all night.

My sister always calls me names,
And wants to blow me up in flames,
My sister always calls me names.

But even though my sister is rotten,
If you're in a muddle,
She will come and give you a big cuddle,
But, she still is rotten.

Lucy Blade (8)
Ashdell Preparatory School

I Have An Otter In Me

I have an otter in me,
Playing noisily,
Rapidly swimming,
Actively defending itself,
Being cautious of other predators,
People watch me fascinated if they have the chance,
But I just ignore them and carry on.

Imogen Stables (9)
Ashdell Preparatory School

The Writer Of This Poem

(Based on 'The Writer of this Poem' by Roger McGough)

The writer of this poem
Is as funny as a colourful clown juggling with 10,000 balls
As strong as a beautiful butterfly fluttering about
As gentle as the waves in the stormy sky.

As fast as a little mouse scurrying along in the long grass
As slow as a snail wandering about the place
As happy as a little girl skipping happily in the sun
As silly as a donkey falling down.

As annoying as a bee swarming around you
As weird as a hyena laughing away in the distance
As noisy as a boisterous trumpet.

The writer of this poem is as clever as can be
But if you need information don't ask me.

Georgia Blagden (9)
Ashdell Preparatory School

School - A Playground Clapping Chant

School, school, what a dread,
Never want to get out of bed.

School, school lessons all day,
Maths and English, no time to play.

Home, home, what a delight,
Oh no homework all night.

Weekend, weekend, no school for two days,
Lie in till 10, no school, yeah!

No school, no school, have a rest,
Have a day out, it's obviously your best!

Lydia Brooks (9)
Ashdell Preparatory School

Don't

Don't bite your nails.
Don't draw on the pillow.
Don't write on your hand.
Don't fight.
Don't be loud for the hamster.
Don't cry.
Don't hit your brother.
Don't forget to flush the loo.
Don't kiss Damian.
Don't punch your brother and sister.
Don't make a mess.

Imogen Parker (8)
Ashdell Preparatory School

Don't

Don't fight with your brother!
Don't bite your nails!
Don't cry!
Don't hurt yourself!
Don't forget to wash your hands!
Don't play karate with your brother!
Don't forget to flush the loo!

Alice Strong (8)
Ashdell Preparatory School

Seasons

In winter the white icy snow falls on the ground
Children laughing and pulling sledges on the white icy snow
Building snowmen, how much fun can you have in winter?

In spring the bright colourful flowers come up after the dull winter,
And the world is a lot brighter and you can see the little yellow chicks,
How much fun can you have in spring?

In summer it is bright and sunny, people eating ice lollies,
People going to the beach and jumping the little blue waves in their
summer shorts.
How much fun can you have in summer?

In autumn children are collecting brown crunchy leaves that have
fallen from the huge tall trees.
How much fun can you have in autumn?

How much fun can you have all year round!

Bethany Fletcher (8)
Barnby Dun Primary School

Me And My Pony

Over the lanes and far away,
My pony and I come out to play.
She's full of fun and never kicks,
She tosses her head and flicks her tail
And eats her carrots in a purple pail.
She and I are such good friends,
I hope this friendship never ends.
I love my pony and she loves me
We are one in harmony.
Over the lanes and far away,
My pony and I come out to play.

Katie Vickers (8)
Barnby Dun Primary School

The Fair

I'm going out today
All my friends will be there
We are going to a theme park
With all the fun of the fair
Hooray we're here, we're just outside
I can see a rollercoaster and a big blue slide
Hustle and bustle people everywhere
Smell of hot dogs and candyfloss in the air
Jump on the roundabout
Round and round
Whoosh, scream, argh, as the roller coaster speeds down.
Quick on the ghost train my friend cried
Better hurry up or we'll miss the ride
I'm scared, it's dark
Oh dear what's that?
It's a ghoul or a ghost wearing a hat
It's coming towards us in the dark and the gloom
I scream it's too creepy
Hope the ride's over soon.
The day is now over
We'll be on our way
Carrying our memories of a wonderful day.

Rachel Grashion (9)
Barnby Dun Primary School

Where Does Sadness Live?

Where does sadness live?

In the trees?
In the breeze?

Over clouds?
Under clouds?

In a prayer?
In a bear?

In a church?
In a silver birch?

Inside a box?
With a fox?

In my house?
With a mouse?

In your heart?
Yes
That is where sadness starts.

Zoe Oxley (8)
Barnby Dun Primary School

Whales

Whales, whales,
What are we like?
Are we black? Are we white?
Don't hurt us, we are nearly all gone,
So please just leave us to live happily along.
The whales' graveyard
Is at the bottom of the sea.
It is caused by you and me.
All that whales want is to be free.
So why can't we just let them be!

Ellesha Curry (8)
Barnby Dun Primary School

King Blue

Whales, whales, swim gracefully.
Whales, whales, live in the sea.
Whales, whales, I love you.
Whales, whales, do you love me too?
Whales, whales, so beautiful and blue.
Whales, whales, who are you?

'Who am I?' you ask of me.
'Don't you know? I'm King Bluey.'
I am a blue whale so proud and so grand,
Please bow with your hand.
In front of me and in front of thee who swim behind me,
You shall do as I say or go away,
For your type of creature kills most of thee who swim behind me.
King Blue have no fear of me,
I'm only here to worship thee,
Who swims in front of me.

Francis Leanne Fisher (9)
Barnby Dun Primary School

The Mad Football Game

Beckham took the shot,
Owen lost the plot,
Seaman flew,
Henry tried to score one too,
Heski hit it last,
Lehman saved it fast,
Smith lost his way,
Scholes saved the day.

Holly Fawley (8)
Barnby Dun Primary School

An Undiscovered World

The world wakes
A thunder of monsters coming my way
I've just woken up
I'm too tired to run and not be squashed
I'm too hungry to move and find food
Do the monsters know I'm here?
The world around me lays undiscovered
I have nowhere to go
Still, metal mountains to be climbed
Still, rusty mazes to find my way out of
More creatures for me to meet
More songs from giant birds to listen to
Still soft mud and hard ground to touch
Still fighting off the monsters to be heard
I don't know where to go
I'm lost I can't be squashed
The world is undiscovered
Then the thunder of monsters of over.
I'm left alone,
I'm safe.

Natalie Brown (10)
Canon Popham CE Primary School

On My Way Home

I am walking in the forest of green grass.
I go to a huge boulder and I can hear birds singing.
I can hear footsteps coming towards me.
The sky is covered in leaves.
The huge spider web scared me a lot.
Bushes and trees were like a cave.
Forests of flowers I had to walk through.
The wind was trying to talk to me but I didn't know
What it was saying.
So now I am on my way home.

Poppy Wickham (9)
Canon Popham CE Primary School

On My Journey Home

On my journey home I can see bright yellow sun.
On my journey home I can see leaves make shapes I never knew.
I can see a path of mud and boulders.
I can see a swamp of water with crocs in it,
Drops of rain falling onto my head.
On my journey home I can see giant ladders.

On my journey home I can smell mints blowing past in the wind,
Sweet pollen blowing me away from living.

On my journey home I can hear birds talk a
Language I do not know.

On my journey home I touch grass to get
Past the wooden swords.

Megan Sowerby (9)
Canon Popham CE Primary School

Home

I walk on as I hear the wind flowing
Through my ears,
I climb the red lighthouse
As I spot a blow out of giants,
I nearly thought I was destroyed.
A scent of lavender flowed through my nose,
Suddenly there, there it was,
An island of wonderful nature,
Which I call home.

Michael Hattersley (10)
Canon Popham CE Primary School

Past The School

As I cross a fortress of grey tarmac,
A giant machine roared past me
Stopping between thin white lines.
Finally my journey begins,
I walk over rocky bumps and trip over green grass.
Past a tree into a huge area,
As I walk on an army of ants march in front of me.
As soon as they pass I heard something in the distance,
A bee with desert yellow and chaotic black stripes.
As I walked through a jungle of grass a massive scarecrow
Reached over me.
Finally I scurried past the school,
I had done it.

Richard Wilkinson (10)
Canon Popham CE Primary School

On My Way Home

Going through the giant trees,
Stepping on the rough boulders,
Looking up in the sky.
I see all the bees buzzing in the air,
Coming at my face like a swarm of thunder.
Me on my way home,
Rushing through the rainfall,
Seeing all the clouds.
I see dragon's eyes glaring at me,
Me on my way home.

Jordan Scholey (10)
Canon Popham CE Primary School

A Long Way Down

Walking around the earth in my big garden
Wandering near never-ending grey rivers
Smelling the lavender as I pass
The sweet smell following me.

Entering the green forest that never ends
Passing the imprisoned snakes
Struggling to get free
Dragons singing overhead.

Going through tall spiky trees
The sound of grass being cut
Echoes in my ear
The sleeping giant silently
Snoring next to me.

James Bellamy (10)
Canon Popham CE Primary School

There Is No Place Like Home

The world is opening up at me,
The light is staring at me through rippled leaves,
I can smell mint leaves but it seems like Sunday dinner,
I struggle to get through the stringy grass,
I pass the lavender, it's so sweet,
Giants are taking a glance at me,
There is an obstacle of nettles approaching me,
I have nowhere else to go except home.

Rhianna Armstrong (10)
Canon Popham CE Primary School

Escaping From Home

Escaping from home nature comes out,
Huge mountains stand before me
And wooden hills on a glade of waves.
Prickly steps from wood chippings
And a boggy smell from a dark room of fear.
Winged creatures chirp in the distance,
As I am walking away.

The future is repeating,
As I walk past nature.
When I look at nature,
Nature looks back.

I cannot escape,
Escape from my home,
Because nature is my home.

Cody Martin (8)
Canon Popham CE Primary School

Waking Up

I awake to a new world,
The lions, their roars are blowing me away,
I'm being watched in the silence of the night,
Snakes are coming out of their lair,
I'm sinking into a mud bath full of enemies,
Planes are flying in the sky with their wings spread,
Grass is cutting me like swords,
My legs are going numb from the long walk and giants
Are fighting over food,
Ice is falling from the cloud painted sky,
It is hail and it's stinging me,
I'm now home in the same tree from where I awoke,
Now I sleep in my cosy bed.

Andrew Stratton (10)
Canon Popham CE Primary School

Going Out To Play

While we're out we see bad bug Billy,
In the high jail lock up.
Walk onto the stepping stones.
Lines of sun making bridges,
But don't take too long.
Feet burning,
But the taste is sweet.

Walk onto the green forests.
You can smell the forests growing,
Future trees are just starting to germinate.
Walk on no turning back,
We aren't alone.
The giants are rushing out in herds.

Quick! Climb up the tree,
Boys are fighting with swords over the princess,
Hide where the swords are growing.
Wait look over there!
The Queen is getting married,
Let's see who it is,
No wait,
It's not a wedding,
It's a funeral,
It's Sid the spider.
It's time to go now,
Run through forests past the gigantic rockets.

Finally I've made it home.

Lois Nicholson (10)
Canon Popham CE Primary School

The Way Through Nature

I can smell the sweet and strong pollen.
Now I worry, as I hear the grass crash together,
As I move on I find myself in a desert of sand.
I come across long and thin snow tracks.
I have been blown onto a noisy running ground.
So curl into a ball hoping not to get trodden on.
I scuttle out of this nosy place and move on.
Not long after I get twisted in long never-ending grass.
I hide under a boulder while a crumbling snowball awaits me.
It was hard but that is the way through nature.

Ruby Bircumshaw (10)
Canon Popham CE Primary School

But I Was On My Way Home

(An Ant's Tale)

I was on my way home
Looking at the beautiful nature on my way
I was barging into daisies which looked like giant fried eggs
But I was on my way home.

I could smell apple mint beside me
I climbed over rocks which were like gigantic boulders
I felt a nettle that really hurt it was like millions of shark's teeth
But I was on my way home.

Now I'm here snuggled in my bed.

Matthew Vann (10)
Canon Popham CE Primary School

Setting Off

My eyes open to see the waking world,
The silky bed of grass rubs against my side.
My first steps into the world I take.
A yellow road stretched out before me,
The speaking birds talk in a language I do not know.
People rushing,
People pushing to get to work on time,
I cross the playground on my own
Me, me stood alone.
The wind whistling in my ear,
As the tangy smell of pollen crawls up my nose.
The cobwebs are abandoned.
No one for them to shelter.
As I wander into the weed cave
An obstacle course of nettles I try to avoid.
I'm heading home, I'm nearly there.
I walk onto an open plane of rock and colours,
The other side is where I'm heading,
My home, my place and the damp soft leaves for my bedding.

Melissa Tasker (10)
Canon Popham CE Primary School

A Bug's Life

I'm walking through the long dusty desert
Hoping I don't get lost
I come to a playground like a sky covered in grey clouds
Up above was a giant spider's web
In front of me now are long sharp needles
Birds are singing
I'm nearly there
My legs are getting tired
And I am getting hot
But at last I am home.

Loren Davison (9)
Canon Popham CE Primary School

The Somnolent Scent

As I crawl over
The crunching grass
My sight gets blocked
By a snowstorm.
I climb over bumpy hills
And enter the valley of rough skin.
Walking a tightrope to the other side,
Suddenly I fall into a wood
Of overgrown flowers.
As I enter my world of nature
People crowd over me.
All I can hear are the birds singing
And the scraping of the children's shoes.
A great eye looking over me.
Leaning through the holes
In the bushes
Making friends with other animals
But the somnolent scent of lavender
Makes me feel calm,
Now I'm trapped in a dark room
I curl up and close my eyes.

Lauren Bruce (9)
Canon Popham CE Primary School

The World

Venturing out I see great grandfather clocks laying down,
I start to climb a colossal mountain,
I struggle to get to the top of the peak,
I see giants saunter across the field as I descend.
Suddenly I see a barred dungeon above me.
I hear the wind lecture at me, that is the world to me.

Alex Woodhouse (9)
Canon Popham CE Primary School

Bug's Life

I'm a bug on a journey,
Walking in the garden through giant nettles,
I am walking on giant boulders.
As I go cars are like giants fighting
I fall into a bunch of flowers,
They are like people
But all I can hear are birds singing
People crawling on the grass like soldiers,
Fighting to get through the crunchy grass
But I am nearly home.

Holly Bint (9)
Canon Popham CE Primary School

The Big World And Little Me

I'm looking up seeing a plague of locust.
The grass like a jungle.
The rocks as big as boulders.
The marks in the wood like a maze.

The sound of the wind makes me struggle to hold on.
The sound is like a never-ending war.
It's like a feeling I've never felt before.
The sound of the birds,
I hope I'm not lunch.

Christopher Mumford (9)
Canon Popham CE Primary School

In My Dad's Beard

In my dad's beard
You'll find stale bogies
You'll find black fingernails
And green toenails in my dad's beard.

In my dad's beard
You'll find teeth
You'll find snot
And maggots
In my dad's beard.

In my dad's beard
You'll find lots of sweets,
You'll find his rotten old feet,
In my dad's beard.

Jody Pringle (11)
Carlton J&I School

My Rappin' Dog Lady

My rappin' dog lady can rap like Slim Shady.
She is slick and smooth, she does whopping dog-doos!
My rappin' dog lady is as moody as a mare
And she can run faster than a hare.
My rappin' dog lady she is the best dog in the world,
I love her so,
I never want her to go,
But sadly she went one year ago.

Brad Allen (11)
Carlton J&I School

My Class

First of all there's me,
Then there's Brad, he's really tall,
Then there's Jamie, he's really small.
Then there's Damien, he thinks he's tough,
And then comes Nathan who eats cheesy puffs.

Now to the girls
First comes Tara, big and strong,
Then Rebecca, her bell goes ding dong.
There's Joanne, she can't keep her mouth shut,
And Jade Berry who loves to tut.

Todd Bailey (11)
Carlton J&I School

Under My Dad's Armchair

Under my dad's armchair
You will find some dead skin
Some mouldy cheese
A half eaten doughnut
Some hair from his chin
A remote control that we thought was lost
You will find some earwax
And you'll find bogies that have hairs in them
That's what you will find under my dad's armchair.

Rebecca Watson (10)
Carlton J&I School

Next

Lining up in neat rows,
Standing two by two,
We all wait in silence
In the quiet and long queue.

But it's not to see a statue
Or to to get into the park,
It's not to see a museum
Or a special work of art.

No we're all lined up in rows
Standing two by two,
Waiting on our school trip,
To use the one and only loo.

Damien Zastepa (11)
Carlton J&I School

My Brother Kyle

My brother Kyle has a big smile
He loves to talk and talk
While he's on a walk.
He's got no style, he can't run a mile.
While he goes for a run,
I sit down and eat a bun.
We all love this brother of mine.
His favourite chocolate bar is a Dime bar.

Garth Halford (10)
Carlton J&I School

In My Dad's Beard

In my dad's beard,
You'll find bits of pizza
Rotten toenails
And dried bogies from his nose.

In my dad's beard,
You'll find earwax,
Mushy peas,
And last year's supper.

In my dad's beard,
You'll find wriggly worms,
Maggots
And fishing wire.

Has he ever heard of a shaver?

Ashley Bowler (11)
Carlton J&I School

My Little Sister

My little sister is a little pest,
She never wants to do a test.
She is thin and always plays with a pin.
My sister likes to play on her bike,
She busted her tyre on a spike.
My sister smells,
She always tries to do spells.

My little sister runs slow,
She likes to play in the snow.
My sister picks her nose
And always plays on my phone.
My sister never blows her bogies
And goes and sees old fogies
And that is my little sister.

Jack Cowell (11)
Carlton J&I School

Under My Dad's Armpits

Under my dad's armpits
You'll find bits of scabs,
You'll find last year's supper
And dried up green bogies.

Under my dad's armpits
You'll find old smelly milk,
You'll find dead cockroaches
And horrible smelly sick.

Under my dad's armpits
You'll find old manky sausages,
You'll find mouldy black meat
And smelly stinky sweat.

Under my dad's armpits
You'll find smelly old earwax,
You'll find old pimples and spots
And last year's old nappies.

And that's under my dad's armpits.

Nathan Kirby (11)
Carlton J&I School

Seaside - Haiku

Rolling waves pass by
As I sit on the seashore
The sea makes a sigh.

Harry Baldwin (11)
Clifton Community Arts School

Insomnia

Through Heaven and Hell,
To conquer the night.

I cannot sleep,
Can't count any more sheep,
They've gone back to the barn.

I cannot sleep,
No more books, they're up in my head,
Quotes swimming around as if in a pool.

I cannot sleep,
Drunk all the milk in the house,
Not a drop to be seen.

Like a soldier I fight,
Through Heaven and Hell,
To conquer the night.

When suddenly . . . *zzzzz*.

Raechelle Little (12)
Clifton Community Arts School

Lovely Holiday

Laying down in the beautiful sun,
Having a great time,
I am having so much fun,
And feel like the world is mine.

I just love going in swimming pools
I always go away,
It is so cool
I'm having a great day.

Tiffany Sterland (11)
Clifton Community Arts School

Sea Poem

What a beautiful day
To go visit the sea.
I always go to the beach
Because that's where I like to be.

To watch all the children
That are playing in the sand
Or even have a donkey ride
While listening to the band.

There are some men that are on a boat
That are right out at sea
They're trying to catch some fish
For us to have for tea.

It's time to go, 'Oh no!' I say
We've had a lovely day
Maybe we can come again
In the school holidays.

Harley Blackham (12)
Clifton Community Arts School

Sunshine! - Haiku

I like the hot sun
The sun is bright and yellow
Smiling is the sun!

Nicole Pimperton (12)
Clifton Community Arts School

Haiku

The heart of my day
Shining in the dead of night
Seeming like magic.

Thomas Watts (12)
Clifton Community Arts School

Victimised

A feeling so bare
You giving me that deadly stare,
My legs are jelly
Butterflies trying to escape my belly,
My head is bleeding, my fingers are sore,
From when you cracked them all, one by one.
Please I'm scared, please no more,
Where are you without your ten men?
It's you with them again and again,
But would my pain have been the same,
If you told your mates didn't have to play the dreaded game,
I wonder what my life would have been without you
Smirking at every chance.
Now I must go, you understand why,
The gang of ten, it is you that made me die.

Emily Passmore-Bailey (11)
Clifton Community Arts School

Sweet Flower - Haiku

Blowing in the breeze
Soft silky petals long green
Bright pollen for bees.

Amy Blacow (12)
Clifton Community Arts School

Bonfire Night - Haiku

Sparking in the night
Tonight is a magic night
Many faces glow.

Abir Hussain (12)
Clifton Community Arts School

Love! - Haiku

Love is in the air
Blossoming love everywhere
What a pretty sight.

Nathan Duckmanton (12)
Clifton Community Arts School

Mountains - Haiku

The mountains are high
Beautiful scenery there
As the clouds go by.

Sophie Davis (12)
Clifton Community Arts School

The Caribbean - Haiku

The blinding blue sky
The warm Caribbean sea
Stretch of golden sand.

Jordan Tracey (11)
Clifton Community Arts School

Happiness - Haiku

A warm feeling spreads
The smile upon your face grows
What a great feeling.

Tanya Gooding (12)
Clifton Community Arts School

Why Do You Make Me Mad? - Haiku

Why are you so mad?
I'd rather see you so glad
It does make me sad.

Kara Sanders (12)
Clifton Community Arts School

Waterfall Magic - Haiku

Waterfall magic
Blue water shines as it forms
Little mini waves.

Kesley Hickman (12)
Clifton Community Arts School

Banana Muncher - Haiku

I am a monkey
Munching giant bananas
Swinging on the trees.

Reece Eblet (11)
Clifton Community Arts School

The Exotic Island - Haiku

The sky is pure blue,
Sea is as still as a rock,
The pimple like rocks.

Sally Morton (12)
Clifton Community Arts School

Ferrari - Haiku

A Ferrari car,
Is as fast as fork lightning,
It zooms with a speed.

Sydhra Bi (12)
Clifton Community Arts School

Simple - Haiku

Beautiful simple
A bird, a flower, a bee
Rather like small me.

Uzma Parveen (11)
Clifton Community Arts School

Sparkle - Haiku

Blue in the night-time
I sparkle in the night's sky
I sparkle all day.

Chantelle Woodthorpe (12)
Clifton Community Arts School

My Brother Is A Terror Now

My brother is a terror now, he moans and groans to watch TV.

My brother is a terror now, he eats nearly all the time.

My brother is a terror now,
He scribbles and says it's a cat or dog.

My brother is a terror now, he plays football at home
And sometimes it hits me.

My brother is a terror now,
He fights me at home and when we go to karate.

I love my brother but he still annoys me.

Aimee Inskip (8)
Drighlington Primary School

Fairy Tales

Witches, wizards, goblets and ghouls,
In fairy tales, you'll find these fools.
Giants, monsters, pixies and elves,
Most of these creatures only think about themselves.
Cheeky, kind, scary and funny,
These sorts of stories they use to make money.
Cool, entertaining, readable and interesting,
This is what you need to think about when
You're writing the next best thing.

Charlotte Mills (9)
Drighlington Primary School

Centre Stage

I'm gay
I'm gay
Jumping around
Getting to the stage dodging the crowd
Holding my awards
For playing my chords
I don't know what to say
I said I wouldn't get it only yesterday
Say something, say something
Please say anything
I don't want to look like a fool
Keep calm, keep cool
Smile and wave
I remembered to have a shave
Got the money
Don't try to be funny
Best day of my life ever
Won't have a better day never.

Sarah Kelley (10)
Drighlington Primary School

The Enchanted Wood

The water rippled in the mystical forest.
The leaves fall like fairies dancing in the air.
The rocks as dark as the night sky.
The grass swaying joyfully in the distance.
The leaves on the trees are as green as a sprout.
The shadows of the trees sparkle in the stream.
The harp is singing in time to the singing of the trees.
The historical water flows down to the sea.

Jack Bentley (9)
Drighlington Primary School

Kitty Cat

I'm cute, I'm cuddly
I'm rolling on the bed
I fell off, I fell off.

I'm soft, I'm cheeky,
I'm curled up in a ball
I'm comfy, I'm comfy.

I'm fat, I'm round
I'm snoozing on the ground
I'm happy, I'm happy.

I'm soft, I'm sweet,
I'm looking for a treat
I'm hungry, I'm hungry.

I'm hiding from the dog
I'm under a log
I'm scared, I'm scared.

I'm small, I'm brown
I'm running all around
I'm tired, I'm tired.
Miaow! I'm going to sleep now!

Lauren Eastwood (10)
Drighlington Primary School

Dogs

I think dogs are the cutest,
Cuddliest, furriest, sloppiest and most adorable
Pets you can get.
But if you're thinking that dogs aren't fun,
Let me explain to you why they are.
You can walk them,
Play catch with them,
But the greatest thing is,
That you can swim in the sea with them.

Thomas Gilpin (9)
Drighlington Primary School

Terrifying Night

I lay in my bed
I just can't sleep
I think there's something there,
I hear it moving,
The curtain twitches.
Silently I get out of bed
And walk towards the door.
The door seems jammed
I'm really scared
I see the toy box open,
I hear a deep breath,
I run towards my bed,
I want to disappear,
A creaky floorboard,
Tempts me to scream
But nothing comes out
I see something coming towards me.
I'm terrified.

Lauren Newsome (10)
Drighlington Primary School

My Sister

My sister is little now
She has got curly hair like spring
And when she speaks she always says silly things.

My sister is little now
She is very cheeky like a monkey.

My sister is little now
She likes playing with Polly Pocket
Dressing up as a fairy.

Keely Runton (8)
Drighlington Primary School

The Thing!

Running down hallways,
Taking a dead end,
The thing chasing me is small, well I pretend,
Banging locked doors,
Letting out a loud wail,
The thing chasing me has a long, fluffy tail.
Peering through windows,
Smashing alarm bells,
The thing chasing me seems to have different smells.
I approach a crossroads
The thing comes up and starts to purr,
Its warm body seems to have fur.
Then it starts to occur,

It was just a cat!

Geena Gaskell (10)
Drighlington Primary School

School

Lovely colours all around,
Dots and gashes on the ground
Helping children learn so much
Maths and science helps a touch
Lots of friends you can have
When you are so raving mad.

All the teachers are so lovely
All of us are too
We hold doors
Say thank you and please
We don't speak Japanese
Or Portuguese
But we are a lovely school!

Louise Raper (10)
Drighlington Primary School

Our Class

In our class things go missing,
So our teacher tells us, hissing.

Someone tiptoes around our school,
Even in our swimming pool.

They move our chairs, pull on our hair
Even say, 'Hello.'

They're invisible and I'm so miserable
How do we end this fast?

They say, 'Boo!' to the kindergarten crew.

I found out why they are,
They drive a big black car.

They're very naughty fairies, they do do do
So I trapped them in my shoe and didn't
Know what to do.
So I'll leave it to school.

Chanice Mallett (10)
Drighlington Primary School

My Cousin Is Young Now

My cousin is young *now*
He is a kid with a beautiful bow
He is a monkey.

My cousin is young *now*
He plays with a ball
He plays with my bobbles.

My cousin is young *now*
He plays with me.

Jadean Mosley (8)
Drighlington Primary School

What I Wonder

I wonder why the world is so big
And I am like a little twig
I wonder why I talk
I wonder why I walk
Why does everyone hate me?
Just because I cannot see
And that is what I wonder of how the world thinks of me.

I wonder why they stop and stare
Life is so unfair.
I feel like I am made out of clay
I am miserable all through the day
I hope it never happens to you
So you cannot feel what I am going through.

Samantha Ingles (10)
Drighlington Primary School

Playground

Playtime is fun
Love to play in the sun
Anybody can sing
Younger children play on the swing
Growl and shout
Run about
Out in the toy cars
Use the monkey bars
Nutty girls and boys
Dinner time toys.

Hetty Sunderland (10)
Drighlington Primary School

The Predator

The predator is five feet long,
The predator hates every song.
When he wants to come out to play,
Everybody else wants to run away.
He decides to come into the house
But instead he kills a woodlouse.
Then someone is in his list,
For the deafening *hissss*.
Now on my own,
All alone.
Near the boiling hot lava
Wearing a balaclava.
The predator is after me,
I know he is.
Just when he finds me,
I'm gone faster than this poem is.

Alice Pearson (10)
Drighlington Primary School

The Lonely Bubble

I am but a lonely bubble
I float around the sea.
But I would never roll on the sand!
Why?
Because there are sharp things in the sand,
Like needles and crisp packets.

Sometimes I go to the edge
Of the sand cliff and wonder
Who would I be if I weren't a bubble?
But I never come up with an idea.

Jay Milomo (7)
Drighlington Primary School

A Fantasy Forest

Trees leaning over looking at me.
I'm just singing dum-da-de
The sun shines through the gaps in the trees
And on them are the lush green leaves.

Long pieces of waving green grass
Hunters searching as I pass.
Then in my way was a great big stump,
I tripped over and fell in a lump.

A little rabbit hops into his burrow,
Then I see a singing sparrow.
The red squirrel hops onto a log,
Now I can't see because of the fog.

The fog has now cleared,
And everything looks weird.
Nothing is stirring
Not even a cat purring.

Timothy Shotbolt (10)
Drighlington Primary School

Animals

Kittens
Your litter tray is your destiny
It's where you sniff and have a wee
When you are done you scratch at the door
As you realise you're leaving litter on the floor!

Piggo
Fat, fat, fat piggy
Trot, trot, I can't run piggy,
You stink, you whiff, you pong,
You do everything wrong
You big lumbering pig.

Charlotte Lyles (10)
Drighlington Primary School

The Dog Language

I'm fat, I'm round,
I'm jumping all around
I'm huggable, I'm huggable,
I'm black, I'm white,
I'm rolling all around,
I'm beautiful, I'm beautiful.

I'm soft, I'm fluffy,
I'm sleeping on your lap,
I'm a sweetie, I'm a sweetie
I'm sweet, I'm cute
I'm eating all my food
I'm crazy, I'm crazy.

I'm small, I'm plump
I'm chasing my tail
I'm dizzy, I'm dizzy
I'm furry, I'm shy
I love to play about,
I'm sleepy, I'm sleepy.
        'Woof, woof' goodnight *zzzzz.*

Ashleigh Henry (10)
Drighlington Primary School

Leeds!

Leeds, Leeds, Leeds, we'll never do the deeds
We're gonna keep on winning until the fans stop singing.
We'll continue winning 6-1 and will always beat the
Mancunian chums.
We're No 1, we're No 1
We'll always beat the Mancunian's bums.
Come on *Leeds,* come on *Leeds*
All the Mancunians just pull out weeds.

Oliver Moody (10)
Drighlington Primary School

The Ponies

There was a bunch of ponies eating hay,
On this bright sunny day.
All was quiet and still
Until they noticed a great big hill.
They clambered up and up,
Until they noticed they'd got stuck.

They tried and tried to get out,
Then one fell and shouted, *'Ouch!'*
Eventually they got out and cried, *'Yes!'*
That was hard it was a pest.
They carried on up and up,
They got to the top and said, 'I need a drink of water in a cup.'

They galloped down,
The came to the bottom and saw a town.
They stood there in amazement,
They all looked like they were in a daze.
They walked on and saw a car,
In the sky they saw a great big star.

They carried on and on,
They came to another field and thought they mustn't have
gone wrong,
They went in the field,
In the corner there were people holding shields.
They stayed in the field all night long,
They agreed to stay in the field with another pony that looked
very young.

Harriet Hanson (10)
Drighlington Primary School

Who Am I?

I love the hay,
I love the jumps,
I love the stables,
And I love the day.
Who am I?

I love getting groomed,
I love getting ridden,
I love getting tacked,
And I love the paddocks.
Who am I?

I have a mane,
I have some hooves,
I am a horse,
So come and ride me today.

Gabbi Pashley (10)
Drighlington Primary School

We'll Never Give In

Leeds, Leeds, Leeds
We'll never give in
Man U's chances are as thin as a pin
We'll win our matches
We'll win our catches
Leeds, Leeds, Leeds
We'll never give in.

Adam Tyas (10)
Drighlington Primary School

My Mum

My mum is young and pretty now.
She smiles all the time.
She is also tall and slim.

My mum is young and pretty now.
She likes to go out.

My mum is young and pretty now.
She likes making cards.

My mum is young and pretty now,
She likes to watch 'The Bill' on TV.

My mum is young and pretty now,
She always smells lovely.

George Booth (8)
Drighlington Primary School

Guinea Pigs!

G row fast
U gly (Not!)
I ntelligent little things
N aughty and a bit cheeky
E at way too much!
A re really cute.

P rance about
I love them
G reat big appetites
S oft and cuddly.

Elsie Smith (10)
Drighlington Primary School

Tropical Truth

The soft sparkling sand squashing beneath my toes,
The clear blue sea rippling silently,
The flame of the orange sun warming up my skin,
Picking the juicy ripe fruit off the tall palm trees,
Smelling the sweet smell of exotic flowers,
Hearing the cry of a distant tribe,
Touching the fur and scales of wild and wondrous animals,
Building a straw house under the shade,
Nobody knows I'm here,
But I am enjoying my stay.

Olivia Jones (10)
Drighlington Primary School

Who Am I?

Marching down the hill, going up and down,
Smelling the freshly baked bread and beautiful sizzling bacon
From the open street
And the beautiful singing on the street,
With a big castle with a horrid man,
Making a silvery sword.

Who am I?
I am a Roman.

Bradley O'Donnell (8)
Drighlington Primary School

The Bogeyman

The bogeyman is creeping up your nose,
The bogeyman is creeping up your nose,
He does it when you're sleeping so nobody knows
The bogeyman is creeping up your nose.

The bogeyman eats everything he finds
The bogeyman eats everything he finds.
No matter how green and slimy he always thinks
They're briney
The bogeyman eats everything he finds.

The bogeyman is gross in every way
The bogeyman is gross in every way
The bogies in his mouth are all called Ralph
The bogeyman is gross in every way.

Adam Stocks (10)
Drighlington Primary School

My Brother

My brother is five now
He shakes his bum into music
My brother is five now
He looks like a devil with his spiky hair
My brother is five now
He's watching Bob the Builder
My brother is five now
He plays football with me.

Daniel Roberts (8)
Drighlington Primary School

Summer

Flowers swaying in the summer breeze
Sheep getting sheared on the farm
Football being played in the park
Children swimming in the pool
Trips to the beach, playing in the slippery, sparkly sand
Splashing in the sea
Making sandcastles
Activities happen like football, tennis, cricket, basketball, netball,
Racing and even long jump.
Visiting museums, just me and my family.

Emma Edwards (8)
Drighlington Primary School

Who Am I?

I can smell the taste of desserts and muffins,
I travel on a long gigantic boat,
Twenty-three people must have big muscles to lift this boat up.
I am wearing a large cloak.
I have long boots.
I live in a temple.
I invaded Britain.

Who am I?
I am a soldier in World War I.

Luke Simpson (8)
Drighlington Primary School

Who Am I?

Sand blowing in my eyes,
Deep dusty sand crawling around my defenceless feet.
Temples all around the sandy whirlwind,
And a herd of fully guarded triangle buildings.
Who am I?
I am an Egyptian god.

Harry Lupton (7)
Drighlington Primary School

Volcanoes

Volcanoes, volcanoes, volcanoes, standing strong and firm.
They stay asleep for centuries, until they feel a burn.
They twitch this way and that,
Until they feel a crack!
They open their mouth and set the lava free.
Splish! Splosh! Splash!
The volcano erupts.
The lava as yellow as the sun.
It went zooming down, knocking everything down in its path of doom.
The city below hasn't seen the show until they hear a blow.
They start screaming and shouting, running away to get away
                                                    from Pompeii.
An hour later the city is toast, the lava has gone away,
Leaving everyone to say, 'Thank goodness we got away, but our city
                                                    could not stay.'

Jordan Hobbah (9)
Drighlington Primary School

The Emperor

I waited for him out on the gate
The guards were waiting too.
There he was in his robe and his crown,
He then spoke words of wisdom
'Thou art the real kings!'
I was proud that my grandad
Was the Emperor of the world.

George Lewis (10)
Drighlington Primary School

Rugby League

Rugby is tough and really rough
You've got to be as tough as steel or else you'll be down and out
Like a shout.
When the whistle blows, be steady at the toes
It goes from first tackle to fifth just like that
The wind blowing like a hurricane
The players as tough as rocks
Their fastest player runs at the speed of light
And then puts the ball down
It's a try!
The crowd goes wild!

Reece Farnhill (9)
Drighlington Primary School

Good Old Spain

If you think it does not rain in good old Spain,
Well look down the drain,
And you'll see a big blob of water
That's bigger than a sumo's daughter.
So go to Spain and get on the plane
And drive down the lane and you will see more rain.
So get back home on a plane and make sure it doesn't rain
But when you get back you will be gobsmacked
'Cause you've just brought the weather with you.

Sam Lupton (10)
Drighlington Primary School

Sharks!

S cary
H ungry for fish
A n animal
R ock hard
K ing of the sea.

Oliver Sullivan (10)
Drighlington Primary School

Magic Classroom

In the middle of the night, in a school of sight,
A classroom is hidden in the dark.
Chairs are glum, the pupils are dumb and no fun is there to be seen.
The headteacher is strict, she looks like a witch,
Thank God school time is over
At twelve o'clock midnight the classroom is not alright
Everything gets over groovy.
The books on the shelves are flying,
The paper on the wall is crying.
The door is singing and the tables are lying to each other.
It turns eight o'clock, the dumb pupils arrive in a flash all of a sudden
The teacher writes a sum on the board and randomly picks on kids
As she opens and closes her eyelids.
The headteacher comes in looking a bit dim as she shouts
                                        at the class,
'Someone in this class broke my glass while I was on the loo,
They smashed my glasses too!'
The children laughed, then in a sudden flash, the class turned dark
And glum, once again.

Shelbi Hoole (9)
Drighlington Primary School

Wild Animals

Animals, animals are so great
Like the tiger prowling through the jungle.
The falcon moving briskly now, sighting its prey
Like the black mamba killing a helpless deer
The shark cutting the water with its sharp, knife-like fin
Like the funnel-web spider eating a juicy mosquito
So silently like the leopard hunting its prey
So loud like a chuckling hyena
So many animals and yet different in each and every way.

Alex Gidley (9)
Drighlington Primary School

Friends

Friends are silly, smart and soothing
They like helping you at school.
You get presents that tell their feelings
They play with you when you're down.
When it's their birthday they invite you to parties.
Then let you sleep the night.
Their smiles will talk.
Their eyes will gleam.
Their hair somehow dances while they speak to you and me.
Friends will help you if you're black or white,
Or if you're blue, green, pink or yellow.
They're always kind and helpful.
Don't be down, play with your friends and you won't have a frown.

Charlotte Thompson (9)
Drighlington Primary School

Crystals

The glowing prosperous crystals sparkling in the night.
The bloodstone shimmers on the rock while the moonlight hits it.
The pearl earrings hanging off its ear.
The aquamarine scuba dives in the sea.
The turquoise gem pulls a funny face while it ties its shoelace.
The garnet's birthday on January 1st.
The amethyst celebrates in February.
So whilst they're celebrating, the evil ruby
Plots an evil plan for world domination.

Harry Ferguson (9)
Drighlington Primary School

Dinosaurs

They eat, they crush, they fly, they kill, the dinosaurs
Some *big!*
Some small
Some downright keen.
Most of them were plant eating machines.
T-rex was a mad meat eating lizard,
12 cm teeth and small little fangs.
Eggs were laid, eggs were eaten, eggs crack.
Little lizards on patrol looking for predators.
Little dinosaurs running round, crocodiles crunching.
Some live in waters, waiting for dinner to swim by.
The male is scared of the female, it might mate with him,
It might eat him, the meteor killed them all.

Luke Sugden (8)
Drighlington Primary School

Dragons

Dragons, rulers of the land and sky,
Raging fires they create.
A legion of dragons to kill anything,
Great beasts they are.
Origins of dragons, not known,
Never to be seen again -
So rare are these fantastic beasts.

Christopher Goult (9)
Drighlington Primary School

Science Lab

All different coloured bottles standing in a row
Some as red as rubies
Some as green as grass
Mr frantically pours some green potion into the blue bottle
Suddenly . . .
Boom!
An extraordinary bang,
Mr's hair stuck up on end like spears,
His face covered in thick black dust
'I think I won't do that again!'
back to the drawing board.
'Aha!' Mr had got it, if you add the funny shaped bottle with
bright pink and then the blue-bright brilliant potion and then . . .
Cor what a smell!
'I give up!' said Mr and he went home, he'll try tomorrow.

Alex Lewis (8)
Drighlington Primary School

Football

Boots echo down the tunnel like horses running.
The players dribble in and out like a slithery snake.
The cross of the ball hits the back of the net like a snap
From a crocodile's jaw.
We're one goal up, cannot afford a rest.
Football, football is the best game while we beat the rest.

Thomas Farrar (9)
Drighlington Primary School

Football, The Final

Oh, it's the Final in Istanbul
Oh, it's a goal
It's a goal alright
54 seconds
The Liverpool fans are appalled with their team's performance
Ref's played the advantage
3 nil at half-time
Stevie's header
3 all at full time
Oh, it's extra time
Oh, it's 3 all
Oh, it's a penalty shoot-out
Dudek saves
Shevchenko doesn't score
Liverpool run across the pitch celebrating
Maroon sparks shot round the players
And gold fireworks outside the stadium
And the pink flares in the crowd
They all go up and collect their medals
Stevie kisses the trophy, won the Final
Having a can of beer and a curry at the pub after the game.

Jacob Rodgers (8)
Drighlington Primary School

Fish

As the golden seahorse swims all day,
A little fish with a tail smaller than an ant.
They are big, small, some bigger than me.
The crystal seaweed walks along the frozen sand,
The old crocked sea ship as piranhas eat all day.

Ben Bridge (9)
Drighlington Primary School

Rugby League

Rugby, rugby, as tough as a cookie
The ball is an oval and as round as a globe
The ball can jump out of their hands
And the person can kick it, it's lucky that it doesn't die.
Hard hits and bones breaking
They get a broken foot so they won't be allowed to hang around
In their hut
The players are strong so they won't do something wrong.
They score a try and get four points, how terrific!
The crowd go wild and celebrate in style.

James Harrison (9)
Drighlington Primary School

Crystals

The glowing prosperous crystal sparkles in the night.
The aquamarine shimmers on the rock whilst the moonlight hits it.
February's amethyst travels around the world
Whereas the topaz sunbathes in the midsummer sun.
The pearl earrings dangle out of her ears.
Now and then the ruby does a double flip
While his wife Lapis Lazuli watches in amazement
The emerald gem pulls a funny face while
He ties his shoelace.

Jasmine Gray (8)
Drighlington Primary School

Rugby

Teams, teams, sprint out the stand
Teams, teams, kick off the cone
Teams, teams automatically speed through the defence
Teams, teams crush and crash in tackles
Teams, teams score perfect tries
Teams, teams do brilliantly high drop goals.
Fans, fans jump up and down
Fans, fans go crazy and mad
Fans, fans plod through the crowd
Fans, fans run up and down
Players, players get sweaty and fast
Players, players are so groovy.

Harvey Dibb (8)
Drighlington Primary School

Who Am I?

Smelling freshly baked bread loaves
Wafting through the open street
The clattering and clanking sound of a blacksmith
Designing an iron sword.
The stomping of soldiers' feet making their way
Through the frosty village.
Who am I?
I'm a Viking soldier.

Adam Banwell (8)
Drighlington Primary School

The Cursed Wild Place

The water became chocolate and melted onto the rough rustic rocks.
The tropical fish danced in and out of the rippling stream,
The magical forest was as colourful as the rainbow.
The clean water rustled, glistened just like stars.
The leaves were swaying and playing with the fish.
The trees were moving and plodding along,
The rippling clean, fresh water began to move towards the bushes.
The trees were as bright as the sun melting like hot lava of a volcano.
Small creatures climbing and chirping, and burping having a feast.
The sound of the water rushing past leaving the standing rocks still
Drifting about.
Massive rock boulders say 'Hello' when you pass by.

Jake Holt (9)
Drighlington Primary School

Friends

Friends are the best thing in the whole wide world.
Best friends are fabulous, they keep your deepest darkest secret.
Best friends are beautiful, starry and surprising.
They are beautiful, red ruby roses singing in the icy breeze.
Friends are fantastic, lovely and gleaming in the bright fiery sun.
Best friends are great.

Katie Elsom (9)
Drighlington Primary School

Night And Day

The night is gloomy.
The stars are twinkling like flashing Christmas lights.
The moon is floating in the deep dark space.
The moon is shining bright like a spotlight.
The sun is bright, boiling and burning hot!
The rain clouds are damp and freezing cold.
The dark clouds have some lightning inside
So stay away or you will get killed!

Elliot Beasley (9)
Drighlington Primary School

Summer

Ruby red roses swaying in the breeze
Bluebells staring at the green trees.
People swimming in the deep blue sea.
Going to the park, just you and me.
People going onto the seaside, building sandcastles by my side.
Going to play hide-and-seek.
Activities going on through the week.
Playing football on the street.

Kelsey McDonald (9)
Drighlington Primary School

Best Friends

F orever friends
R eally kind and caring
I let my friends sleep at my house
E ach and everyone should trust each other
N o disagreement with anyone
D ifferent games we like to play
S o friends always keep their promises to you.

Kelly Wilkinson (9)
Drighlington Primary School

Holiday

Holidays are exciting for children and adults
We spend the whole year looking forward to these wonderful
Weeks of freedom
No school, no work
We zoom through the sky in the aeroplane
When we land, we get popping ears
The sun is bright, my body feels warm
Can't wait to dive in the cold water of the pool
With my new holiday friends.

Jade Hustler (8)
Drighlington Primary School

Friends

Friends are the best thing in the whole wide world,
Best friends they never tell your secrets
Never tell, never say,
They are always by your side and
Always come to your house
When you ask them, they come.
They are the most beautiful, blooming friends
You could ever have.
They are beautiful red rubies.

Jennifer Cable (9)
Drighlington Primary School

Volcanoes

Volcanoes erupting like a thunderstorm
Fireballs shooting in the sky
Lava destroying everything in its way like bullies
Lava bubbles blowing up in the cloudy sky
Blowing up the sky
The people all around screaming in the town.

Mac Taylor (9)
Drighlington Primary School

The Mystical Forest

The water of the stream strolled merrily through the dark
                                        lonely forest.
Tropical fish dance in the stream.
Fish jump peacefully up and down the small rushing waterfall.
Animals hide up in the depths of the forest.
The sounds of the trees rustle in the wind and break the silence
Of the dark night sky.
The breeze of the wind makes the calm, peaceful water ripple.
Every so often tropical fish jump up and down and make a small
Flash, like lightning in a stormy sky.

Lauren Taylor (9)
Drighlington Primary School

Skateboards And Roller Skates

Skateboards and roller skates zooming round Morley Park.
High back flips everywhere
People falling here and there, skateboards sliding down the ramp
Doing grinds everywhere
Spinning fast like a blade
The sparks coming from the grinds on the roller skates.

Jordan Stretton (9)
Drighlington Primary School

The Deep Dark Forest

The trees rustled as the shallow stream passed silently
                                        through the forest.
Rocky banks stand proudly where grasses grow with waterfalls
Splashing in the water.
The birds sing as they leave their nests.
Suddenly the peace is shattered by trees falling in the distance.

Adam Stevens (9)
Drighlington Primary School

The Never-Ending River

The trees whisper sounds waving at the sparkling sun,
The sound of falling water can be heard from a nearby waterfall.
A small island breaks the water into two paths,
Birds are singing songs of magic in the swaying trees,
Fish dance merrily in the roaming river.
The trees were hiding the glistening light.
Beautiful plants grow wildly at the other side.
Vines dangle from trees making a mystical sight.
The river seemed never to end.

Cain Harniess (9)
Drighlington Primary School

The Magic Wild Forest

The brightness of the trees shimmer as they swish in the sun.
The harp plays gentle music as the birds sing softly in the breeze.
How the lake smashed like a car crash.
As the sun shines on the river,
The lake glistening in the sparkling daylight.
As the leaves fall, the wind blows.
The clouds move up above as the wind blows away the cobwebs
Created by nature's friend.

Lucy Solomons (8)
Drighlington Primary School

The Mysterious Forest

The trees were waving to us as I walked by the enchanted forest.
The water welcomed the harp right at the edge of the forest.
The tune was talking to me,
Something just dropped in the clear, sparkling, glittering water.
The grassy field reached out like a stable,
The harp was smiling, rocky rough rocks seemed to move the
musical melodic noises.

Liam Bailey (9)
Drighlington Primary School

My Grandpa

My grandpa likes gardening now
He has a big garden.

My grandpa likes gardening now
He plays dominoes, he always gets the double six.

My grandpa likes gardening now
He walks up big hills with me.

My grandpa likes gardening now
He has big blue eyes.

My grandpa likes gardening now
But he doesn't act his age.

George Bentley (7)
Drighlington Primary School

The Enchanted Wood

The whistling wind gliding through the trees,
The rippling water catching the breeze,
The old trees waving, dropping off leaves,
That come fluttering down,
Like fairies dancing in a castle.
Historical creatures climbing about chirping and eating,
Having a feast,
A strange man looking in the trees,
Wow! he thought, *that's brilliant,*
Whoopee!

Reece Matthews (8)
Drighlington Primary School

The Mystical Jungle

The trees standing like soldiers guarding.
A small river twisting and turning through the trees.
A harp waiting to be played on the riverside.
A man silently walks through the unknown jungle looking around
Like he is puzzled.
Leaves falling off the trees like angels floating down to Earth
And extinct animals run past like a flash.
Rocks standing like statues.
The trees like camouflage disappear into the depths
                              of the mystical jungle.
Fish red as fire dance to the sound of the water rippling.

Ben Mitchell (8)
Drighlington Primary School

The Misty Forest

Birds glide over the mystical wonders of the forest.
Leaves fly from trees like aeroplanes taking off.
The misty water sparkles as cold as ice.
The frosty forest moves softly and quiet as an empty room.
The hush of the harp plays to the sound of the whistling wind.
The fish are as red as fire to the music of the breeze.
The rustic rocks are as slithery as a snake shimmering in the
Wet light of the sun.
The shy animals are as still as a statue camouflaged by the trees,
Watching as the whispering water strolls by.

Calum Hepworth (9)
Drighlington Primary School

The Magical Forest

The birds are singing high and low,
Swooping through the whispering trees.
The fish are swimming down below,
Swishing by the chattering toads.
There stands the golden harp playing to itself
A magical tune that whistles in the wind.
The trees blow in the wind as the man and the dog
Walk past the shadows of the forest.
Quiet it goes as the moon slowly rises and the sun sets.
Another day gone, another to come.
The magic still dancing in the darkness of the night.

Jennifer Davies (9)
Drighlington Primary School

Thing In The Swamp

An abandoned hare plays a merry tune, dancing trees,
Walking frogs jumping from rock to rock.
Calm and wonderful, a place so peaceful that you could sleep.
So quiet like a musical with no noise,
A winding river bank with jumping fish and waterfalls,
Ducks swimming slowly.
Birds flying high like an aeroplane,
Leaves falling like snowflakes from the sky.

Andrew Bailey (9)
Drighlington Primary School

The Shadowy Wood

The shadows were swaying along with the wind,
The ripples were rippling in the shape of litter, two big circles,
The waterfalls were splashing with their flow,
The ripples sounding like they were echoing.

Amelia Grey (9)
Drighlington Primary School

The Mystical Forest

Bushes sway merrily from side to side
As a slight breeze flies by in the light of the summer sky.
The sound of the water rushes past, leaving the soft still rocks,
Drifting slowly by.
The leaves are falling from the nearly bare trees,
Already floating on the roof of the rippling water.
Huge rock boulders smile as you pass them by.
Tropical flying fish dance out of the water, splashing the stream
In a blink of an eye.
A man in the distance looking very puzzled, as a magic silver harp
Plays by itself on a gigantic rock beside the river on a misty and
                                                    foggy night.

Gregory Barker (9)
Drighlington Primary School

The Wild Wood

The forest was calm and beautiful and you could hear mystical
Creatures and extinct animals rustling through the trees.
The stream rippling, pushing fish forward,
Plants and trees swaying in the breeze.
Trees falling in and out like a triangle,
As the water hit the raining rocks, it burst off them,
And the frogs jumped in the camouflaged water.
You could see the frog spawn at the bottom of the river
As their mother frog came and checked on them.

Luke Austin (9)
Drighlington Primary School

My Grandpa

My grandpa is fun now!
He is very, very artistic,
He paints portraits of me.

My grandpa is fun now!
He watches TV, mostly army stuff,
Watches all day long.

My grandpa is fun now!
He plays snooker,
Pot, pot, pot.

My grandpa is fun now!
He likes reading stories
Horror, action, adventure.

My grandpa is fun now!
And he doesn't act his age.

Robbie Gaskell (7)
Drighlington Primary School

My Dad

My dad is funny now
He plays with me.

My dad is funny now
He likes Miller beer.

My dad is funny now
He likes playing rugby.

My dad is funny now
But he doesn't act his age.

Oliver Wilkinson (8)
Drighlington Primary School

My Sister

My sister is fifteen now
She has hair as soft as feathers and
She likes watching TV.

My sister is fifteen now
She is as pretty as a rose
And she gets me told off.

My sister is fifteen now
She has nice clothes and she always goes out
With her friends.

My sister is fifteen now
But she doesn't act her age.

Ellie Carney (8)
Drighlington Primary School

My Dad

My dad is old now,
He has jazzy hair.

My dad is old now,
And likes playing snooker and pool.

My dad is old now,
And likes riding his bicycle.

My dad is old now,
He likes dogs now.

Sam Hanson (8)
Drighlington Primary School

My Nana

My nana is fifty-four now
Her hair is as dark as a room with no lights.
She wears glasses that are really small.

My nana is fifty-four now
She likes cartoons and when we play the Xbox
She sometimes wins
And I am an expert.
She washes my clothes all the time
As soon as I come round.

My nana is fifty-four now
She watches the news all the time
And CSI, also Law and Order.

My nana is fifty-four now
But she doesn't act her age all the time.

Brandon Byrne (8)
Drighlington Primary School

My Dad

My dad likes arcades now
When he plays arcade games,
The toys come out.

My dad likes arcades now
He has built a racing car.

My dad likes arcades now
He is going on holiday with me to Spain.

My dad likes arcades now
But he doesn't act his age!

Declan Smith (8)
Drighlington Primary School

My Dad

My dad is young now
He likes cars like mad and football.

My dad is young now
His head is as bald as a hard-boiled egg
But inside millions of things are going on.

My dad is young now
His feet go snip, snap like a pair of scissors.

My dad is young now
But he doesn't act his age.

Georgina Holmes (8)
Drighlington Primary School

My Dad

My dad is on new shifts now
I get to see him much more.

My dad is on new shifts now
We go bike riding every Saturday.

My dad is on new shifts now
He is a very bad singer.

My dad is on new shifts now
And it has just been his birthday.

Jack Day (7)
Drighlington Primary School

Santa's Train

Santa's train comes out at night
It glows in the very bright light
Presents and packages delivered at your door
Even though the parents are poor
Whistling and singing, the elves do
As they check the parcels and the crew.
Letters from teachers asking for the kids to behave.
Letters from cows asking for hay.
Letters from children asking for it to be Christmas Day.
Letters from grandparents begging not to pay.
Letters from aunts asking for pants.
Letters from pigs asking for wigs.
Letters from spies asking for wives.
Letters from people all round the world.
Letters from girls asking for pearls.
All dropped off at Santa's shop
There and then he grants all your wishes
Here comes your cooked turkey *mmm . . .*
Delicious.

Sasha Beardsley & Bethany Clark (10)
Drighlington Primary School

The Transporter

At the station you could hear a slight *toot, toot*
And the conductor shouted, 'All aboard!'
Then the animals screeched with fear
As the wheels screeched on the rusty railway tracks,
All was silent and then . . .
Juga Jug, Juga Jug, Juga Jug, Juga Jug, Juga Jug, Juga Jug,
And it got quieter and quieter and quieter,
As the train disappeared in the distance and the track quietened.
The train was gone, *whizz, whizz, whizz,* past the trees
And the cattle and fields, ponds and birds,
And before we knew it, we were in Spain.

Callum Hargraves & Jack Bradford (10)
Drighlington Primary School

The Way To New York

From San Francisco to New York
We travel night and day
We delivery mail to rich and poor
We pass through mountains, moors and villages.
Fast ahead I puff my smoke
Behind my shoulder my driver shovels lumps of coal
Into my mouth.
Faster than lightning, faster than blinking.
The brakes are screeching as I stop.
The mailman gets out and takes a lot
And delivers to the people who wait.

Bradley Pickles & Abigail Housecroft (9)
Drighlington Primary School

My Dad

My dad is old now but he doesn't act thirty-six
Because he plays rugby with me and kicks it over the posts
From the half-way line and always gets it over the posts.
He also loves playing pool!

He's got dark black hair and brown eyes and his lips are white.
Next my dad's building a car and it is fast because I've been in it.
My dad's favourite PlayStation 2 game is Simpsons Hit and Run,
Grand Theft Auto Vice City and San Andreas,
As well he likes playing football with me.

Kieran Boulton (8)
Drighlington Primary School

The Train

The whistle toots
The brakes screech
The sights pass and
The wheels creak.
The grass sways as the flowers dance
As we go in the tunnel it goes pitch-black
As we come out, the dazzling sun is shining on the chrome
Funnel.
The people wave,
The birds fly,
The ducks swim,
And the kids cry.
People gabbing
The conductor blows his whistle,
Stopping at stations one by one,
At every one someone gets on and off.

Jack Wilson (10)
Drighlington Primary School

Who Am I?

I sail in a ship, a long one about 15 metres long,
Going hunting for seals and animals like birds,
Going home to eat and rest,
The ship I sail in is so long you could fit one hundred people in it.
Who am I?
I am a Viking soldier.

Marc Willis (8)
Drighlington Primary School

The Great Big Train

The great big train,
Goes through lots of rain,
The train crossing all the borders
Taking lots of orders.
The whistle, crying,
But inside it's frying,
It went through some towns,
Some people made frowns.
There are letters for the rich and the poor,
And whoever lives next door,
Some flames are dancing,
Some flames are prancing,
Fluffy clouds coming out of the funnel,
But down it, it looks like a tunnel.

Robert Jones (10)
Drighlington Primary School

Who Am I?

Marching through the frosty sky with snowflakes
Dropping from the draughty blue sky.
I can hear a fire blustering through the sky,
I can hear a blacksmith, designing an iron sword,
I can hear a blacksmith stomping through the village,
Big, black and rough,
I can hear soldiers echoing through the sapphire sky.
Who am I?
I am a Saxon from Sutton Hoo.

Jake Carney (8)
Drighlington Primary School

The Deserted Wood

The harp softly played as mystical fish danced to its
                                  enchanting music.
Shadowy water glistened with eyes that stared at me in the distance.
The glistening water rippled softly in the moonlight.
The leaves fell silently to the floor.
The misty banks with its exotic plants swaying quietly
                                  in the soft breeze,
Trees fell in the distance crushed by lightning.
The rocky river seemed to go on forever.
It was as magical and enchanting as a wonderful wizard.
The historical trees swayed merrily.
The brilliant breeze rustled the soft leaves.
A young boy is mesmerised, 'Wow this is amazing!'
The roof of the waterfall flows swiftly along the dazzling damp
                                  blue river.
The greasy banks are home to many creatures.
Fish jump peacefully in the waterfall and fire around the river.
The forest is truly amazing.

Michael Smithson (9)
Drighlington Primary School

Who Am I?

Flying through the icy air,
Hearing the slam of the bombs,
Hearing the hot bacon popping and sizzling in the pan
For my breakfast,
Who am I.
I'm a pilot from the Second World War.

Jordan Sullivan (7)
Drighlington Primary School

The Mystical Shadow

One comes the other goes,
The misty sky showed as the clouds disappear.
You may think it's all over,
Others say it's only just beginning.
It'll never be over not now the trees are camouflaging themselves.
The mysterious creatures travel the ground.
The rippling stream flows as magical and enchanted as a wizard.
An invisible person, they say it plays with the harp making soft
Whispering sounds.
There's an old man and his dog that comes down to the stream
Every day.
We don't know what's going to happen.
The shadowy stream is as quiet as a lonely village.
One day there was a storm, a storm worse than ever,
That's when it all ended.

Grace Daji (9)
Drighlington Primary School

Who Am I?

I march through the frosty street,
There's clanking from the blacksmith's,
It's a scary place,
The ships look like dragons.
Who am I?
I am a Viking.

Benn Sharp (7)
Drighlington Primary School

The Wild Rainforest

The thunder smashes down as the waterfall fills with lovely
sparkling water.
The sound of the wind rustles in the air.
The branches of the trees seemed to reach out and touch the stars
As the harp played mystical music in the bustling breeze.
The leaves were falling in the distance as the sounds of voices
Echoed through the rocks.
The boulder near the sparkling stream seemed to groan as the logs
Floated and bashed against their rough edges,
Continuing to flow with ripples rushing past,
Caused by the windy sky.

Jodie Mitchell (9)
Drighlington Primary School

The Mystical Forest Within

The forest within was a very bad place
Lots of strange things happening in here.
They say the forest has a magical curse
The trees with listening ears
Strange animals rule the land, never to appear,
People have gone there, but always disappear.
Nobody go, a quiet warning whispers through the trees.
The scent of fear drifting in the breeze.

Chris Hanson (9)
Drighlington Primary School

The Magic Forest

Leaves fall from trees like fairies happily dancing in the daylight.
The misty air shines as bright as the moon on Hallowe'en.
The magical harp softly plays as the trees sway in the
                                    sudden breeze.
The waves of the rushing river silently crash against the roughness
Of the rocks and hit the ground like thunder.
Plants gently rock to the music of the harp,
Beating a rhythm of the enchanted forest.
The harp slows down as the waves get heavier,
With the wind blowing through the harp's strings.

Sarah Cowles (8)
Drighlington Primary School

My Grandad

My grandad
Likes football,
He nearly watches every football match
In the world.

My grandad
Likes bowling,
He's won quite a few matches.

Timothy Tomlinson (8)
Drighlington Primary School

Who Am I?

I defeated the Romans,
I invaded in 410AD,
I got defeated by the Vikings
I sailed across the Atlantic Ocean.
Who am I?
I am a Saxon warrior!

Libby Wilson (7)
Drighlington Primary School

Who Am I?

Soldiers marching through the village.
Footprints in the snow crackling in the ice.
The scraping of the blacksmith.
Fighting of the men and soldiers.
The swishing smell of the baked bread.
The squawking and singing of the blackbird,
The washing of the ladies,
A girl called Chloe was singing a beautiful song.
The clanking of the noises in the village,
Designing a silvery iron sword,
Who am I?
I'm a Roman soldier.

Keely Cooper (8)
Drighlington Primary School

I Am!

Marching through the frightened streets,
With blacksmiths working hard,
The swords are huge and long,
Frightened people stay inside
Captains are giving frightening orders.
Who am I?
I am a Saxon warrior.

George Williamson (8)
Drighlington Primary School

Who Am I?

Marching through the ice-cold streets,
Smelling the ripe fruit,
Feeling my sword, hard as rock,
Feeling my cold leather suit.
Who am I?
I am a Roman soldier.

Lila Kara-Zaitri (8)
Drighlington Primary School

Who Am I?

I can hear the explosion,
The fire comes past my face,
I feel the wind on my face,
The pilot talking to me from the front.
Who am I?
I am a World War Two bomber.

Jobe Rennard (7)
Drighlington Primary School

Who Am I?

The bang of a gun and a bombshell,
Wind breezes across my face while grenades blow up our base.
Daisies get blown up or stood on.
Who am I?
I am a soldier from the Second World War.

Jack Walker (8)
Drighlington Primary School

Who Am I?

I hear the loud clanking of the hard workmen working,
The horrible shouting of the king ordering the servants about,
The nasty screaming of the poor people fussing about everything,
Who am I?
I'm Queen Elizabeth the First.

Abigail Waller (8)
Drighlington Primary School

Happiness

Happiness is as green as the long green grass
It sounds like children running and playing
It tastes like delicious lemonade running down my throat
It smells like bubbling eggs in a frying pan
It looks like a colourful rainbow
It feels like a wonderful day
It reminds me of my friends.

Simon Lovitt (8)
Hawksworth CE Primary School

Happiness

Happiness is a loving Mum and Dad
It sounds like children playing in the playground
It tastes like sweet chocolate pie
It smells like the smell of bluebells
It looks like a sweet strawberry
It feels like a baby's hand
It reminds me of laughing at a joke.

Ella Lefley (8)
Hawksworth CE Primary School

Fear

Fear is black like the dark sky
It sounds like someone screaming
It tastes like blood
It smells like rotten milk
It looks like a ghost
It feels hot and fizzy
It reminds me of being stung.

Garth Darwin (8)
Hawksworth CE Primary School

Darkness

Darkness is black like the gloomy midnight sky.

Darkness sounds like drums beating to a dreaded death.

Darkness tastes like badly burnt brown bread,

Darkness smells like slippery, slimy pond weed,
Darkness looks like dark creeping shadows, climbing up
The spiny walls.

Darkness feels like the wind ruffling up my hair.

Darkness reminds me of my dead pet in Heaven.

Amy Turk (9)
Hawksworth CE Primary School

Fun

Fun is yellow like the sparkly sunshine.
It sounds like a baby giggling.
It tastes like smooth strawberry ice cream
Dripping off a cone.
It smells like a red rose swaying in the breeze,
It looks like a shiny blue dolphin jumping in the ocean,
It feels like my first hug from my mum,
It reminds me of six weeks off school.

Daniel Holt (9)
Hawksworth CE Primary School

Love

Love is pink like fluttering blossom in the air,
Love sounds like a harp playing in the summer breeze,
Love tastes like crisp pink icing on a heart-shaped cake,
Love smells like Jelly Babies just come out of the packet,
Love looks like a pearl gleaming on the sandy seabed,
Love feels like someone tickling my feet,
Love reminds me of swimming in the salty sea.

Elizabeth Heard (9)
Hawksworth CE Primary School

Love

Love is pink like blossom hanging on the tree
Love looks like a heart growing on a flower
Love feels like hugs and kisses given from my mum and dad
Love tastes like melted chocolate in my mouth
Love is everywhere
Love sounds like newborn babies in a nursery
Love smells like lavender perfume
Sprayed on my mum
Love reminds me of visiting the Queen
Love is everywhere
Love is in the air
Love is everywhere.

Lizzie Ayre (8)
Hawksworth CE Primary School

Laughter

Laughter is as blue as the big blue sky
It sounds like my lovely Mum saying good morning
It tastes like ice cream running down my chin
It smells like steaming hot toast
It looks like a tickling feather
It reminds me of a funny clown.

Sam Chilvers (8)
Hawksworth CE Primary School

Darkness

Darkness is black like the leather on my shoe
It sounds like a monster under my bed
It tastes like cold and lumpy rice pudding
It smells like a monster's armpits
It looks like a man with a black cape
It feels like goosebumps growing on my arm
It reminds me of when I walk down the corridor
On my own in the dark.

Joseph Mountain (8)
Hawksworth CE Primary School

Anger

Anger is like red boiling hot lava running down a rocky valley.
It sounds like a hurricane swirling and whirling.
It tastes like boiling hot steam and hot spicy chilli.
It smells like burning hot fire.
It looks like a bright orange tiger with a fierce face.
It feels like a steaming hot pan.
It reminds me of nightmares.

Cameron Scott (8)
Hawksworth CE Primary School

Fear

The colour of fear is black like the night sky,
It tastes like off milk
It smells like the sewer
It looks like a terrifying ghost
It feels like a hairy spider
It reminds me of bad dreams.

Rhys Austwick-Holland (8)
Hawksworth CE Primary School

Laughter

Laughter is the cat's first yawn
Laughter tastes like a chocolate sponge pudding
Laughter smells like fresh air in the morning sunrise
Laughter sounds like children laughing.
Laugher looks like children having fun on holiday.
Laughter feels like love.
It reminds me of hugs and kisses from my family.

Amy Swales (8)
Hawksworth CE Primary School

Love!

Love is red like a bursting volcano
Love looks like my hair swaying in the wind
Love tastes like sweets in my mouth
Love smells like a fire burning
Love feels like a bird in its egg
Love reminds me of my cat, sat by the fire
Love sounds like a baby's first cry.

Isabel Simmen (8)
Hawksworth CE Primary School

Sadness

It sounds like the night sky
It tastes like the wind
It smells like the salt in the sea
It feels like the air going through my hand
It reminds me of my mum.

Mitchell Wellman-Brown (8)
Hawksworth CE Primary School

Fun

Fun is yellow like the soft sticky sand.
It sounds like children laughing.
It tastes like creamy chocolate.
It smells like the grass when it's just been cut.
It looks like it's fantastic
It feels like fun
It reminds me of my mum.

William McLaughlin (8)
Hawksworth CE Primary School

Darkness

Darkness is black like the rooftops
It sounds like the wind blowing on the trees.
It tastes like mint fresh cold.
It smells like chocolate melting.
It looks like a black cave.
It feels like magic in me.
It reminds me of nasty people.

Ella Sagar (8)
Hawksworth CE Primary School

Laughter

It sounds like a puppy's first bark
It tastes like chocolate sauce
It smells like strawberries
It looks like a puppy's first food
It feels soft like cuddles
It reminds me of kisses.

Francesca Smith (8)
Hawksworth CE Primary School

My Body

My hair is like the sea I suppose,
It curls and waves with the wind.
My eyes look like two pools of blue,
When they spin they look like whirlpools.
My nose looks like two tunnels,
Leading up to my eyes.
My mouth is like a big cave
That opens and closes when I tell it to.
My arms look like branches,
That sway from side to side.
My fingers are like spider's legs,
Each one long and wriggly.
My legs are like huge tree trunks
They hold the rest of me up.
My feet are a bit like frogs,
Always jumping up and down.

This is my body you see.

Ashleigh Brain (11)
Inglebrook School

My Body

Like a clock, I have a face
My face has eyes like sparkling gems
Then comes my nose in the middle space
The sound from my mouth tells you it's me
With two arms which move like branches on a tree
I can make my fingers wriggle like little worms
And use them to pick up many germs
Like me, a table without its legs would fall
My feet give me balance to stand straight and tall
My body, like an engine, keeps me going day to day
But unlike it, I move to walk and play.

Rachel Connell (11)
Inglebrook School

A Poem About Me

My eyes are like a sort of marble, that can see day and night.
My head is like a football, which I'd kick into the sky.
My neck is like a support, holding my head high, so it goes right
Into the sky, a bit like a pylon holding the wires high into the sky.
My ears are like little stations, picking up signals from all around.
My legs are like big long branches, from a weeping willow.
My fingers are like spider's legs, bobbing up and down,
And my wrist is like a screw, holding on my hand.
My hand is like a machine, picking things up and putting them down.
My mouth is like a vacuum, sucking bits of food in,
And my feet are like a chair's feet, taking all of the strain,
Then when I sit down, they briefly relax.
My brain is like a computer, working things out.
In fact my brain is working out things now.

Ellis Birkby (11)
Inglebrook School

My Body

My head is like a big acorn
With messy hair on top
My eyes are like footballs rolling around
My mouth is like a black tunnel that never closes
My fingers are like worms wriggling around
My arms are like branches that aren't very long
My legs are like towers making me tall
My feet are like leaves sprouting from a branch.

Thomas Copley (11)
Inglebrook School

Ideas From My Paintbox

Today
I have come to say
Would you like to see
My paintbox?

Red is sweet wine
The bright roses that bloom
Hearts which give you love
The crunchy apples we eat.

Blue is the splashing sea
The sky on a summer's day
The school uniform I wear most days
Dolphins leaping about in the ocean.

Orange is the skin on a pumpkin
The tasty sweets that we like
The sunset as it starts to sink
The cheesy topping on my food.

Gold is the Queen's crown
The stars shining at night
Pound coins chinking in my pocket
The star shining on my work.

Parice Fenning (10)
Inglebrook School

Ideas From My Paintbox

Today
I have come to say
Would you like to see
My paintbox?

Red is the apples that we eat,
The blood pouring from a cut,
The cherries dropping from a tree,
The hearts on birthday cards.

Green is the juicy grapes we eat,
The colour of a million eyes,
The bamboo that pandas eat
The prickly stalk of a rose.

Orange is the beautiful sunset,
The pumpkin on Hallowe'en
Cheese on a sandwich,
The tulip on a spring day.

Black is the ink from a pen
A stallion galloping wild.
A ripe plum plucked from a tree
A taxi in our capital city.

Francesca Payne (9)
Inglebrook School

Ideas From My Paintbox

Today
I have come to say
Would you like to see
My paintbox?

Green is the grass ready to be cut
The treetops swaying to and fro
The grapes about to be eaten
And eyes gazing all around you.

Blue is a door you walk through
A drain pipe leaking water
The chair you sit on day by day
And water gushing by.

Black is a blackboard ready to be cleaned
The night sky turning into morn
A horse you ride around a field
And a taxi tooting its horn.

Orange is the sun starting to set
And cheese with crackers to eat
A pumpkin ready for Hallowe'en
And best of all an orange sweet.

Ben Newman (10)
Inglebrook School

Ideas From My Paintbox

Today
I have come to say
Would you like to see
My paintbox?

Red is roses growing on a bush
Ketchup that is on the children's chips
The crunchy juicy apples waiting to fall
Blood that is spurting out of a wound.

Black is the taxis running up and down
The mystery of a dark winter's night
The horse galloping through the fields
The ink dripping out of a pen.

Green is the leaves on the trees
The bamboo swaying in the breeze
The settee my friends sit on
The menacing eye of an evil beast.

Blue is the colour of my uniform
My chair I sit on every day
The sky on a bright summer's day
The waves hitting the shore.

Kate Lovatt (10)
Inglebrook School

Ideas From My Paintbox

Today
I have come to say
Would you like to see
My paintbox?

Black is the burglar's galloping horse
A cold frosty winter's night
The board on which the teacher writes
The blots on a page of writing.

Red is the English Rose
The squirting blood of a child's nose
The blazing fire of an old London street
The Christmas stocking hanging at my feet.

Green is the juicy pear
Summer's leaves growing on the trees
Grassy fields filled with crops
The farmer's tractor starting up.

Orange is the daffodil's trumpet
The freshly picked orange
A smiley faced pumpkin
And newly grown spring tulips.

Megan Stephens (9)
Inglebrook School

Ideas From My Paintbox

Today
I have come to say
Would you like to see
My paintbox?

Pink is the curly tail of the pig,
The juicy flesh of a fig,
A blushing girl who has fallen in love,
And the sunset in the sky above.

Grey is the smoke from burnt toast,
The fur of a rabbit as it burrows at the coast
It is the lead of the pencil we use every day,
And the pigeons in the air flying away.

Black is the colour of type in books,
The shadows that come and play with us,
The blackboards we use at school,
And also the colour of my school shoe!

Red is the jam inside a cake,
The strawberries that taste yummy and great.
Cherries on a tree that blow and sway,
And the hearts of people that pump all day.

Georgina Freeman (9)
Inglebrook School

Limericks

There was a young girl who was sad
She was really ugly and bad
She visited Leeds
She said, 'That's what we need.'
That naughty young girl who was sad.

There was once an old woman in red
She spent most of her days in bed
'This bed is my home
So leave me alone,'
Said that lazy old woman in red.

There was once a young boy from Mars
He ate loads of chocolate bars
He ate all day
Till his stomach gave way
That fat, spoilt, young boy from Mars.

Karan Pugal (10)
Inglebrook School

Limerick

There was an old lady from Leeds
Where there were lots of bees
She had lots of honey
And made lots of money
That rich old lady from Leeds.

There was an old man from Leeds
Who planted lots of flowers and trees
He began in the sunlight
And finished at midnight
That hard-working man from Leeds.

Charlotte Barker (10)
Inglebrook School

Limerick

There was a young girl from York
Who sat down to have a talk
She sat on her lawn
She stayed there till dawn
The young girl from York who did talk.

There was a young man from France
Who made up a little dance
With a girl that did sway
He practiced all day
That very elegant young man from France.

Rowena Jenkins (10)
Inglebrook School

Limericks

There was an old man from Spain
Who somehow was always in pain
He went to some abbots
Who gave him some tablets
Which relieved that old man from Spain.

There was a young man called James
Who dearly loved to play games
One day he played Scrabble
With a noisy rabble
That brilliant young man called James.

Luke Whitaker (10)
Inglebrook School

Limericks

There was once a lady from Barnsley
On her fish she liked to eat parsley
Then she found a bone
And she did moan
That shocked young lady from Barnsley.

There was an old lady from York
She loved to eat lots of pork
She got very fat
And sat on her cat
That silly old lady from York.

Leah Bygrave (10)
Inglebrook School

Limericks

There was a young boy from York
Who learned how to walk and talk
He talked all day
He was born in May
This chatty young boy from York.

There once was an old tabby cat
Who grew bad-tempered and fat
He slept all day
In the farmer's hay
That idle, bad-tempered, fat cat.

Nick Howarth (10)
Inglebrook School

My Fierce Anger!

My stomach burning,
Steam coming out of my ears
My veins boiling like they're going to burst
My mouth is blowing fire,
Because

       My dog . . .

The weather starting a thunderstorm,
My hair on fire
My heart pumping like it's going to scream

       Ate my . . .

My eyes as red as blood,
My nostrils are bigger than the teachers,
I feel like I want to scrape the moon.

       Homework . . .

Isobel Leaverland (8)
Manston St James Primary School

The Boy

Whenever the sky is darkening
Whenever the lights are out
All night long the wind starts blowing
He rides out and about
Then the snow starts to fall to the ground
Then they all come to turn the night around.

Whenever the wind is nice and soft
Whenever the wind changes
There I stay frightened in the loft
And there are no rangers
Then I stay in the loft with my toys
There is a boy making a lot of noise.

Luke Hemming (10)
Park Road Primary School

Red Is . . .

Red is a fire
Being wet by a hose.
Red is a cherry
The colour of a rose.

Red is a strawberry
It looks so yummy
Red is an apple
And it rumbles my tummy.

Red is a ruby
I think it's mine
Red is the sunset
It has a nice shine.

Red is lipstick
It is the best
Red is a poppy
Better than the rest.

Red is a tomato
Nice and ripe
Red is a brick
A different sort of type.

Red is Mars
Very, very hot
Red is a crab
Moves like a robot.

Joshua McCann (9)
Park Road Primary School

The Sea!

The sea gives a reflection on my face.
They are white horses rushing in the sea.
Sweeping seaweed on the sand.
Waves crashing on the shore.
Tides coming in to my feet.

Zainab Hafejee (10)
Park Road Primary School

What Is Green?

What is green?
Grass is green
A park in-between
The leaves are green on the tree tops
So high and then say goodbye.
The grapes are green
They are very clean
But I think they are mean.
What is green?
A pear is green
But there is a queen in-between.
Hills are green full of grass
But it is going fast
And it is half past.

Bilaal Valla (9)
Park Road Primary School

Bonfire

It is the sun sparkling
It is a giant oven
It is the sound of nuts cracking
It is a million worms wriggling
It is a person burning puffing smoke
It is lots of fireflies lighting up the night
It is fingers flicking in the sky.

James Aston (10)
Park Road Primary School

The Water

See the ripples through the puddles,
Shallow, gentle and still.
Feel the water rushing through your shoes,
As you stand in the stream.
See your reflection in the river,
But don't go too near or you'll fall in with a scream!
See the tremble of the ocean,
Hear the motion of the crying seas,
And watch the really big waves,
Raging through the sea!

Sarrah Ammar (10)
Park Road Primary School

Red

Red is a heart beating like mad
Red is a rose my mum had
Red is a strawberry sugary and red
Red is the sunset coming up from bed
Red is lipstick shining on your lips
Red is a cherry like a plum with pips
Red is fire burning bright
Red is a poppy who said, 'What a sight!'

Lauren North (8)
Park Road Primary School

Yellow

Yellow is the custard
Poured in my plate.
Yellow is the mustard
The one I hate.
Yellow is the cheese
That mice eat.
Yellow is a daffodil
That seems so neat.
Yellow is the sun
Shining bright.
Yellow are the stars
Giving light.
Yellow is a banana
My favourite fruit
Yellow is a light bulb
That matches my suit.

Ashia Zaneb (9)
Park Road Primary School

What Is Green?

What is green?
The leaves are green on the tree tops,
So high they fall off.
Green is a frog in the pond hopping all around.
Green is a nettle waiting to be found.
When they find them they get stung.
What is green?
The grass is green with flowers growing in-between.

Huzaifa Motara (9)
Park Road Primary School

Red As A Rose

Red is the rose
Dazzling in the sun
Red is a cherry
On a delicious bun.
Red is an apple so ripe
Red is the sunset that everyone likes
Red is a poppy
Look at the beauty
Red is a strawberry that is so juicy.

Lucy Hodgson (9)
Park Road Primary School

Star

Leaves are green, floating in your dream
Green tennis balls, they're round, like one pound
Green apples are tasty and they're juicy.
Green frogs are in the pond all day long
Green hills are steep and still
Mean and tasty very green as cucumber
Grass is green
Feels tickly with bare feet.

Atif Farid (9)
Park Road Primary School

Green

A frog is green
Hopping around.
A crocodile is green
Eating fish making a crude sound.
Green are leaves that are high,
Under the bright blue lovely sky.
Green is the rain dripping, dripping.
An iguana is green, slowly creeping.
Green are the leaves floating high above the sky.
Green is a pear making a lovely crunchy sound,
Going all around.
Green is a grape juicy and sweet.
Green are eyes looking for heartbeats.

Shazaib Hussain (9)
Park Road Primary School

Dolphin

Blue is a dolphin jumping in the sea.
Blue are bluebells sitting at the bottom of a tree.
Blue is a blue tit soaring through the sky.
Blue is a whale which shoots its water up high.
Blue is a sapphire dazzling in the light.
Blue is the rain which will ruin a kite.
Blue is an ocean which opens far and wide.
Blue is a piece of sticky blu-tac,
Oh yes, it can hide!

Rabeeah Ammar (9)
Park Road Primary School

Yellow

Sunflower is yellow
Soft as a marshmallow.

The yellow skin of a banana
It looks like its pyjamas.

Sun is yellow
Shining bright
That gives us light.

Yellow olive oil
You can boil.

Nadia Asif (9)
Park Road Primary School

What Is Red?

What is red?
Red and juicy apples
Red soft cherries
Red soft and juicy strawberries
Red blood that spreads everywhere
Red roses smell very nice
Red sweets taste very nice
Red lips are soft and red.

Mohammad Tayyab Ashraf (9)
Park Road Primary School

What Is Blue In The World?

Blue is the whale
Big but not pale
Blue is the dolphin
That is female or male
Blue is blu-tac
Sticking to walls
Blue is the sea
That has a lovely call
Blue are eyes
My mum makes me scared
Blue is marbles
That can be red.

Talha Daji (9)
Park Road Primary School

Red

Red is an apple juicy and sweet.
Red is a rose dozing around.
Red is blood passing through your body.
Strawberries are sweet
Just good for your treat.

Hamzah Islam (9)
Park Road Primary School

Yellow Is . . .

Yellow is a daffodil
Swaying in the breeze.
Yellow is the sun
Way above the trees.
Yellow is the stars
Shining through your knees.
Yellow is a sunflower
Making you sneeze.
Yellow is a lemon
Making you queeze.
Yellow is a light bulb,
Big and bold.
Yellow is olive oil
Smelly and old.
Yellow is the moon
Shining and gold.
Yellow is butter
Mellowy and gold.
Yellow is a banana
Just been sold.
Yellow is cheese
Feed it to your mouse.
Yellow is rice
You might find some in your house.

Jack Robinson (9)
Park Road Primary School

What Is Blue?

What is blue?
The sea is blue
Salty and deep.
The fish leap into the water
Bright and light.
The sea looks like a kite.

Kieran Bennett (9)
Park Road Primary School

Red

Red
Is a fire
Engine, same
Colour as a rose.
Red is my bobble like
A clown's nose.
Red is a poppy that has no shape
As a brick. Red is blood unlikely
To be lipstick. Red is a royal carpet
Same as my favourite cars. Red is
Fire burning hot like Mars.
Red is a ruby like a cherry.
Red is a crab that lives
At the beach. Red is
A big fat delicious
Scrumptious juicy
Berry.

Iqra Amjad (9)
Park Road Primary School

Red

Red is a fire engine glowing bright.
See its light shining through the night.
Red is a cherry, so nice and tasty
Hear it crunch and see it hanging way up high
Red is an apple, hear it crunch,
See it in the fruit bowl once.
Red is a royal carpet set out for the Queen
And she is really mean.
Red is a sunset when the sun falls down
And it goes down and down until it touches the ground.

Chloe Hammill (8)
Park Road Primary School

What Is Red?

What is red?
Blood is red going through your veins to your brain to make it work.
What is red?
Strawberry is red juicy sweet strawberry.
What is red?
A rose is red shining bright in the sky.
What is red?
A sunset is red that I have never met.
What is red?
A cherry is red, juicy sweet shiny cherry.
What is red?
A lipstick is red that you put on your lips
That makes your lips move.
What is red?
A poppy is red lying relaxing on his bed.
What is red?
A queen's carpet is red
When the Queen walks on it the floor and the doors open.
What is red?
Mars is red, sweet like chocolate bars.

Safina Bi (9)
Park Road Primary School

Henry Moore Poem

Henry Moore's sculptures are wonderful for . . .
All the curves and carves, huge and large
And smooth right to the stone.
Inside or outside everyone loves his abstract figures.
Mostly he would use bronze and stone all still,
Stiff and smooth he brought them all to life!

Gabrielle Renavent (9)
St Joseph's RC Primary School, Castleford

Henry Moore

Sculptures: stony figures,
Maybe large, maybe small,
As hard as titanium,
Yet works of art.

Sculptures: round and fat,
Square and thin,
World famous sculptors have done these for years,
That's right, they're sculptures.

Stone: large, small,
Chiselled into to make sculptures,
Smooth or rough,
Stone is a sculptor's material.

Wood: sometimes used for houses,
Sometimes used for barns,
Sometimes used for cow sheds,
Sometimes works of art.

Bronze: metal that's green and brown,
Henry Moore's favourite material for sculpting,
Heated to be moulded,
Into works of art.

Evan Lynch (10)
St Joseph's RC Primary School, Castleford

Anger

Anger is red like blazing fire
It sounds like men being tortured
It tastes like spicy chilli
It smells of burning cars
Anger feels like diving off rooftops
Anger is a burning fire.

Jordan Cairns (11)
St Joseph's RC Primary School, Castleford

Henry Moore

(Henry Moore made many sculptures he made them from bronze, stone and clay. He made many figures. He and his sculptures are famous and yet he's from Castleford. Some of his sculptures are made from wood and are very large)

Sculptures curved and huge
Bronze and cold
Smooth figures
In the outdoors.

Sculptures wood and stone
Large and cold
As he hammers away
In the great outdoors.

Sculptures stiff and still
Silent and posed
Never moving
In the great outdoors.

Louise Farr (10)
St Joseph's RC Primary School, Castleford

Happiness

Happiness is rosy red like a blooming flower
It sounds like laughter
It tastes like chocolate
It smells like a bunch of roses
Happiness feels like a cuddle from my friends
Happiness is a blooming flower.

Fiona Appleton (11)
St Joseph's RC Primary School, Castleford

A Poem About Henry Moore

Sculpture: bronze and smooth
Standing solid and unmoveable
It's a lovely sight to see
In the great outdoors.

Sculpture: stone and cold
So smooth and artistic
And it looks majestic
In the outdoors.

Sculpture: wooden and curved
Rounded as a roller coaster
And as curvy as the sea
In the outdoors.

Hannah McGrath (10)
St Joseph's RC Primary School, Castleford

Henry Moore Sculptures

Sculptures bronze and smooth
Shaped and rigid
Gigantic hard figures
In the outdoors.

Moulding brings the art to life
Making it smooth and curved
Very cold and solid
In the great outdoors.

Mark Newson (9)
St Joseph's RC Primary School, Castleford

Love

Love is kindness.
Love is summer blue sea.
It sounds like a tambourine shaking gently.
Love tastes like Mrs Ellison's flapjack.
It smells like sweetest honey.
Love feels like a special cuddle from my mum.
Love is the best feeling ever.

Jordan Fort (11)
St Joseph's RC Primary School, Castleford

Anger

Anger is like a red devil
It sounds like a volcano about to erupt
It tastes like a hot chilli pepper
It smells like burning wood
It feels like being thrown off a cliff
Anger is violent.

Liam Beck (10)
St Joseph's RC Primary School, Castleford

Anger

Anger is red like the Devil
It sounds like smashing glass
It tastes like a very hot chilli
It feels like being thrown into a fire
Anger is a devil.

Jack Farr (11)
St Joseph's RC Primary School, Castleford

Sadness

Sadness is grey like
An old gloomy graveyard.

It sounds like threatening
Thunder and tastes like ink.

It smells like a dead body
And feels like darkness.

Sadness feels like pouring rain,
Sadness is gloomy.

John Adey (10)
St Joseph's RC Primary School, Castleford

Anger

Anger is red like blood,
It sounds like glass smashed to smithereens,
It tastes like mouldy, out of date food,
It smells like rotten eggs,
It feels like a devil inside me,
Anger is violent!

Bethany Jones (11)
St Joseph's RC Primary School, Castleford

Love

Love is red like a fluffy heart.
It sounds like soft breathing
It tastes like a jelly bean.
It feels like soft cushions
Love is red like a fluffy heart.

Rachel Gray (11)
St Joseph's RC Primary School, Castleford

Animals - Haiku

Horses march a mile
Carry me along the shore
Breeze blows through my hair

Deafening dogs bark
Alone on a winter's night
No reply comes back

Simple cats lie down
Waving their tails about
Just hanging around

Wild animals roam
They're grazing in the meadows
Birds peck the tiny seeds.

Connor Mulvaney-Walls (11)
St Joseph's RC Primary School, Castleford

Happiness

Happiness is as red as strawberries
It feels like a warm summer day
It sounds like birds singing sweetly
It tastes like a chocolate bar
It smells like sea splashing on me
Happiness is as red as strawberries.

Bethany Goodson (11)
St Joseph's RC Primary School, Castleford

Happiness

Happiness is blue like a glistening sea
It sounds like colourful birds chirping along
It tastes like sweet juicy apples
It smells like soft red roses
It feels like shouting loudly in joy
Happiness is like the glistening sea.

Katie Smith (10)
St Joseph's RC Primary School, Castleford

Sadness

Sadness is like a silent, glittering sea
It sounds like chiming silver bells
It tastes like sour sweets
It smells like crumpled, dead flowers
It feels like being eaten inside
Sadness is like a silent glittering sea.

Natalie Tracey (11)
St Joseph's RC Primary School, Castleford

Anger

Anger is red like a blazing fire
It sounds like a volcano erupting
It smells like beer burning
It feels like boiling oil, bubbling inside you

Anger is a blazing fire.

Joshua Gallagher (11)
St Joseph's RC Primary School, Castleford

Hatred

Hatred is a black dark night,
It sounds like booming music in your ears,
It tastes like a volcano erupting inside you,
It smells like mouldy cheese,
It feels like a black hole sucking you in,
Hatred is a chill running down your spine.

Amy Howley (11)
St Joseph's RC Primary School, Castleford

Whistling Wind

Wind whistles through branches
Cold icy air runs straight through me
From the door wind whirls.

Sat in my warm chair
Watching ice melt from my window
Waiting for summer.

My cat is laid down
Next to the fire - warm and snug
Close my eyes to sleep.

Wind whistles through the branches
Cold icy air runs right through me
From the door wind whirls.

Grace Brookman (11)
St Joseph's RC Primary School, Castleford

Sadness

Sadness is blue like a filling of a blueberry pie
It sounds like rain drumming on the rooftops
It tastes like a cold cup of coffee
It smells like a burning burger on a barbecue
Sadness feels like you're shrouded in mist
Sadness is blue like a filling of a blueberry pie.

Edward Maskill (11)
St Joseph's RC Primary School, Castleford

Insects - Haiku

Insects creep and crawl
Insects hunt around our house
Crawling creepily.

Kirsty Newman (11)
St Joseph's RC Primary School, Castleford

Anger

Anger is dark red like a flaring fire
Burning rapidly,
It sounds like a steam train
Charging on,
It tastes like a sour lemon,
It smells like molten lava,
Anger is dark red like a flaring fire
Burning rapidly.

Nathaniel Greening (10)
St Joseph's RC Primary School, Castleford

Hatred

Hatred is scarlet like a face of fury
It sounds like a stealthful soldier ready to kill
It tastes like fresh blood
It smells like sewage
Hatred feels like being tossed and turned by the ferocious sea
Hatred is the face of fury
Hatred is violent.

Reef Bray (10)
St Joseph's RC Primary School, Castleford

Love

Love is red like a fiery flaring heart,
It sounds like the atmosphere filled with laughter,
It tastes like sugared strawberries in melted chocolate,
It smells like fresh roses,
It feels like love that you always need,
Love is a fiery flaring heart.

Jessica Sharpe (11)
St Joseph's RC Primary School, Castleford

Love

Love is like a silky pink heart,
It sounds like a heartbeat racing,
It tastes like sweet candyfloss,
It smells like a bunch of roses,
It feels like your first kiss,
Love is like Heaven.

Amy Rumney (10)
St Joseph's RC Primary School, Castleford

How James Gerrard Became A Buckingham Guard

There was once a Buckingham guard,
His name was James Gerrard.
He started off in the army,
Even though he was barmy.
Then he became an officer,
His squad always obeyed and shouted, *'Yes Sir'*
He then became General Gerrard,
James now owned a couple of guards.
He earned a great deal of money,
Until things were not as funny.
The Germans were trying to take over,
So James set off to Dover.
His enemies were very mean,
So he went to see the Queen.
The Royal Family was kind,
Then James began to find,
He was working as a guard.
What an adventure and this is
The story of how James Gerrard
Became a Buckingham guard!

Christian Walton (11)
St Joseph's RC Primary School, Wetherby

I Pushed Myself And I Did It

Bang!
The gun goes off as I look on at the track spread out before me,
I start to run and know that physically I'm ready, but mentally
                                    I don't think I am.
A girl overtakes me and I feel angry as well as very discouraged,
I'm telling myself to work harder, so I pick up the pace taking the
                                    lead again.
I can feel the first sign of pain flaring straight into my side,
The bell rings and I'm relieved to know that there's only one more
                                    lap to go.

Everybody's accelerating even faster than a car engine,
I'm so tired now and each stride is making me weaker and weaker.
I surge onwards, and as I approach the last one hundred metres
I'm giving it all I've got. But, the question is: am I giving it enough?
I've nearly made it and I'm battling it out with another girl.
It's so close now, but I give it one last surge as my foot crosses
                                    the line . . .

I've won!

Emily Legg (11)
St Joseph's RC Primary School, Wetherby

Home Is Behind

Home is behind,
The big world ahead,
And there are many paths to tread,
And though we pass them by today
Tomorrow we may come this way,
And take the hidden paths that run
Towards the moon or to the sun.

Through shadows to the edge of night,
Until the stars are all alight.
Our home is behind the world ahead,
Forget about that,
We'll wander back to home and bed.

Maeve Anderson (10)
St Joseph's RC Primary School, Wetherby

Wing Wang Wong

(Based on 'On The Ning Nang Nong' by Spike Milligan)

I remember, I remember
A noise the weirdest one
It went, *Wing, wang, wong*
Then disappeared
And then it all began.

I was on the Wing, Wang, Wong
Where the toucans go bong
And their wings really shatter, clatter
You would wonder what's the matter
When you visit the Wing, Wang, Wong.

Before I knew it I was back in my bed
With the toucan's noise inside my head
I've never heard that noise but I hear
That the Wing, Wang, Wong is somewhere near.

Then one night it crept upon me silently
And a little light shone very brightly
I knew at once I was off and going
Knowing Wing, Wang, Wong was the place I was heading.

I was on the Wing, Wang, Wong
Where the tigers go tong
And their claws wibber, wabber, woo
You would wonder what to do.

As normal I was back in my bed
And I lay down my tired head
I wondered when I would return again
Was the Wing, Wang, Wong waiting for me.
I don't know, I'll wait and see.

Sophie Crayford (11)
St Joseph's RC Primary School, Wetherby

I Hate My Best Friend

Tom who lived next door,
Was my all time best friend.
But suddenly our friendship
Came to a sudden end.

His dad had to work
In a city far from me.
So they moved to America,
To live in Washington DC.

When he left me I was lonely,
As lonely as can be.
So I started to hate him,
For what he did to me.

This is how our friendship,
Came to a sudden end.
This is how I came to hate,
My very own best friend.

Adam Waterfield (11)
St Joseph's RC Primary School, Wetherby

Alone

The sun was shining through the trees,
The wind was whistling on the breeze,
My hair was blowing around my face,
With no one walking in my wake.

I was alone that sad, sad day
Looking over the glistening bay,
With no one there to hear my call,
Under that tree, so very tall.

I remember my parents saying farewell,
It was then that I sadly fell,
Into the sea with waves so high
That I left the Earth with a sigh.

Rachel Keighley (11)
St Joseph's RC Primary School, Wetherby

Classroom Chaos

Claire, put that away,
I don't have time for this today,
Liz, sit on your chair,
And stop playing with your hair,
James, give me that,
And take off your ridiculous hat,
Sam, get up off the floor,
Please someone close that door,
Lauren, maths book out,
Don't make me shout,
George, what's five times eight?
And stop asking your friend Kate,
Liam, sit still,
Don't lean on the window sill,
Tom, now's not the time to rest,
In lessons we have to try our best,
Rose, don't throw Ben's pencil case,
And wipe that smirk off your face,
Alice, put your pumps on your feet,
And keep the cloakroom tidy and neat,
Hannah, will you listen to me,
And get a plaster for Joe's knee,
You will all be pleased to know,
That now it's time for us to go!

Rosie Baker (11)
St Margaret's CE Primary School, Leeds

Differences

Broccoli, carrots, chips and beans
Starving begging human beans
Medicine, plaster, a healing pill
Battered, dying, extremely ill
Gifts and presents, receive or give
Empty-handed they do now live
Crops and vegetables will always grow
There, clean water will never flow
Hotels, flats, houses or schools
Starvation and poverty always rules
For our country the future is clear
The only water they have is the droplet of tear
Here, we have no fear or fright
There they search for life day and night
We are the lucky ones of the Earth
They still cry, ongoing from birth
Make a difference save a life
You will not regret the sacrifice
After all *you* live in a safe place
Why not put a smile on someone else's face.

Emily Hall (11)
St Margaret's CE Primary School, Leeds

Cats

There was a little cat,
Who wore a great big hat,
He was straightening his hairs,
When he tumbled down the stairs,
He gave a great big cry,
We could not see why,
Then he thought there was a net,
But he went to the vet.

Emma Jeffries (11)
St Margaret's CE Primary School, Leeds

The Real Playground

As I walk into the playground,
I look at the climbing frame.
It opens its jaw,
While the bars struggle to keep it tame.

My eyes drift to the slide,
It looks as slippy as green slime.
The slider is sure to be eaten,
OK, not this time.

The swing bear's zoo chains,
The seat is enclosed behind the chain.
It cries for help and rescue,
Then swings back and forth in pain.

One throw of a ball and I'm painfully hit,
Straight in the head and soon the climbing frame's
No monster, neither is the slide, the swing is no zoo,
That's what's really in our playground,
The truth is there's evil all round.

Elizabeth Roughton (11)
St Margaret's CE Primary School, Leeds

My Dream

S hoes, wedges, heels, platforms
H ats, sun, floppy, straw
O odles of dresses, blue, green, purple
P erfume, gold, silver, blue, red
P ens, paper, pencils, sharpeners
I ndoor shops or out
N eon lights glittering, sparkling in the sun
G irls, boys, gents, ladies, staring in amazement and wonder

So much to buy, so little time!

Rebecca Daw (10)
St Margaret's CE Primary School, Leeds

My Worst Nightmare

The immensely huge monster crashed against the rocks,
Which were the only thing standing between me
And my worst nightmare,
Without warning it fleetingly descended away
From the docks,
Rolling and crashing back comes my worst nightmare.

It came at full pelt as if its descent had
Only been to create a run up,
There were no longer rocks between me and my
Worst nightmare,
It roared as it approached me, I could smell
Its salty breath as it came close up,
Closing in fast, nearly at me, was my worst nightmare,
The sea.

Sarah Roughton (11)
St Margaret's CE Primary School, Leeds

Footballers

Van Nistelrooy is the boy
He makes the crowd shout for joy
Harry Kewell is so cool
Will never be the goalie's fool
Michael Owen keeps on going
Goals from him always flowing
Robinson Paul with the ball
Is the best keeper of them all
Roy Keane is so mean
Tackling people is his dream
Gary Neville is a real devil
He always plays at the highest level
Mark Viduker is good at snooker
Boro' think he's super-duper.

Rachel Akhondi (10)
St Margaret's CE Primary School, Leeds

The Newborn Foal

Small, small foal
Chestnut brown
Like a shiny conker.

The shaking legs
Trying to stand up
Blinking eyes looking around.

In the swaying green grass
The little foal
Is starting to walk.

Long bushy tail
Long smooth mane
Shining hooves glisten in the sun.

Calm as it is
Not too proud
This little foal
Is growing up.

Hannah Walton (10)
St Margaret's CE Primary School, Leeds

Swimming

Costume on
Goggles on my head
Teacher Mr Don
Shouts - ready.

Splash I'm in
Never-ending pool
Start to swim
Speeding up.

Swim like a fish
Different strokes
My only wish
An Olympic swimmer.

Freya A Chappell (10)
St Margaret's CE Primary School, Leeds

Endangered

Endangered creatures,
Swimming around
Poachers coming
Don't make a sound.

Endangered creatures,
Creep on the beach
Bury their eggs
From poacher's reach.

Endangered creatures,
Flapping with their fins
Fast as lightning
Poacher wins.

Endangered creatures,
Brown and shaken
Poachers ensnaring
Till all are taken.

Endangered creatures
Look at you
The poachers win?
It's up to you.

Molly Pickering (9)
St Margaret's CE Primary School, Leeds

World War II

Fighting in World War II
The great big man lost his shoe,
He didn't know what to do,
So he shot a weird guy from Peru,
The guy landed on the soldier's shoe,
Hooray he'd found it, now what to do?

Helen Wilson (11)
St Margaret's CE Primary School, Leeds

Racehorse

Spotless, white starting gate,
Brushing my shaking legs,
Sound of the crowd, roaring,
Bell went, we're off,
Galloping, galloping, galloping round a track.

Glossy, strong, muscled thoroughbreds everywhere,
We were coming for the first post,
Everything a blur,
My mind whizzing,
Galloping, galloping, galloping round a track.

Winds streaming through my hair
Booming in my face, hooves all around,
Kicking up dirt as they go,
Coming up front,
Galloping, galloping, galloping round a track.

Neck and neck,
Thunder sweating, dripping from him,
Sweat pouring
Dirt flying, not seeing
Galloping, galloping, galloping round a track.

Thunder flew over soft ground,
Both horse and human hearts beating fast,
Racing down the last stretch
I can see the line,
Galloping, galloping, galloping, round a track.

Nearly there,
Over the line,
First
Dreams, reality
Joy.

Sophie Baker (9)
St Margaret's CE Primary School, Leeds

I Never Want To Return

In the mill, the hunger the sorrow,
The overseer is threatening me,
All I want is a hot meal,
I feel so very tired,
I want to go, escape and never return.

In the mill, the hunger the sorrow,
Hunted by machines like bears,
All I want is to fall asleep,
I feel so very hungry,
I want to go, escape and never return.

In the mill, the hunger the sorrow,
The hunger of the machines waits for me,
All I want is to go home,
I feel so very scared,
I want to go escape and never return.

The mill owner strides up and down
He sees me,
He takes his whip and beats me,
All I want is to have a rest,
In the mill the hunger the sorrow.

Jacob Brown (10)
St Margaret's CE Primary School, Leeds

Anger

Anger is like red, hot tomato soup

Anger has no taste to it, just burning steam filling
Up your mouth.

Anger smells like smoke clogging up your nose.

Anger sounds like a boiling kettle screaming like a lost kid.

Anger feels like burning hurting your hand.

Daniel Ramsden (9)
St Margaret's CE Primary School, Leeds

Poetry Despair

Oh this isn't fair,
It's put me in deep despair,
I can't write my poem!

I really wish I could,
'Cause I honestly think I should,
I wish I was like my brother,
Owen.

He can write a lovely long rhyme,
Out of his head, line by line,
Like a wonder poet.

He can help me when I'm stuck
And write it in my poetry book
In ten seconds flat, he's written it!

Oh this really isn't fair,
I'm trying to take so much care,
I'm making a mess.

Hang on
That rhymes,
And they're poetry lines!
I've written my poem.
Yes!

Lizzie Lloyd (9)
St Margaret's CE Primary School, Leeds

Love Is Like . . .

Love is like a romantic dinner,
Love tastes like red wine,
Love smells like chocolate,
Love sounds like calm and peaceful music
Love feels like a big hug.

Amber Tallentire (10)
St Margaret's CE Primary School, Leeds

Style Trial

'Style Trial' says you cannot
Wear woolly gloves and hat when it's hot
Wear checked shirt and striped trousers
Wear camouflage green and turquoise blue
Whatever you choose, 'Style Trial' shows through you.

'Style Trial' says you can and must
Not let clothes show any dust
Tops absolutely must be in season
Trousers should *never* lag behind
Whatever you choose 'Style Trial' will mind.

'Style Trial' says to be in fashion
Must always be your very first passion
Fussing about what to wear
When you shop you shop for style
But for clothes advice go to 'Style Trial'.

Kate Blackburn (10)
St Margaret's CE Primary School, Leeds

I Look

When I go to bed
I always take a peek
To see what's there waiting
Till I fall asleep.

And they will strike when
I am dreaming away in the
Middle of the night.

I will awake in such a fright
But still it's all in my imagination,
What dreams,
Such dreadful sight.

Christopher Caress (10)
St Margaret's CE Primary School, Leeds

Shark Attack

Turtles, dolphins, fish
In a peaceful sea
Danger is near
Sharks.

Like a deadly spear
Killing all in its path
Watch out
Massive vicious eyes
Looking for prey.

Dolphins playing happily
Oh what joy
Until
Shark attack
Death, disaster
The water turns
Red.

Alexander Sherriff (10)
St Margaret's CE Primary School, Leeds

Anger Of Fighting Fear

Anger is red like fire,
It tastes like hot burning chilli,
It smells like warm smoke rising,
It looks like boiling sun,
It sounds like crackling fire,
It feels like melting in the night.

Charlotte Marsden (10)
St Margaret's CE Primary School, Leeds

Camping Woes

When we go camping . . .
My mum complains about,
Ready-made food,
And tripping over guy ropes.
But she loves
Old rickety boats,
And catching trout.

When we go camping . . .
My brother complains about,
Animals, midges, flies
Scaredy-cat!
But he loves
Swimming in rivers
And climbing trees.

I however,
Love surfing at the beach,
And fossil hunting.
I complain about . . .
The tent with holes
But we all hate
The broken showers!

Lois Davies (10)
St Margaret's CE Primary School, Leeds

My Love

Love is pink like bright lipstick
Love tastes like people kissing
Love smells like your loved one shaving
Love looks like a teddy holding a heart
Love sounds like people laughing
Love feels like being lovely and warm in bed.

Kiera Verity (10)
St Margaret's CE Primary School, Leeds

Boats, Boats

Boats, boats up and down the harbour
Cargo, passengers, cars and trucks
To washing machines and fridges,
Boats, boats up and down the harbour
Racing fish to the sea and catching them for tea.
Boats, boats up and down the harbour
The passengers looking at the dolphins as they
Are sailing out to sea.
Boats, boats up and down the harbour
The captain says, 'We're out to sea,'
To all the passengers and crew.
Boats, boats up and down the harbour
Coming into different lands in just a few hours
Boats, boats up and down the harbour
Little trips, big trips, the passengers are happy
Boats, boats up and down the harbour
Coming back home, it was a wonderful trip.

Darius Baghban (10)
St Margaret's CE Primary School, Leeds

Fighting Fear

Fear is all your worst enemies
Fear tastes like mouldy rotten bananas
Fear smells like the smoke from a burning fire
Fear looks like wild horses rearing
Fear sounds like angry roaring people coming towards you
Fear feels like being lonely.

Emma Lumb (9)
St Margaret's CE Primary School, Leeds

My Fear

My pain feels like a snake
Sucking the blood out of me
My pain hears my stomach
Growling like a dog
Hungry for food
But only the bitter taste of dust.

My pain feels like a whip
Hitting me really hard
My pain smells like the mill owner's warm lunch
I am not glad to see it because I don't get it.

My pain looks like the machinery monster
Crunching me like a fly, very, painfully.
My pain tastes the rancid food,
Given to the pigs if we don't eat it.

My pain feels like a tiger
Grinding me down
It feels like a heavy weight
On top of me.

My pain sounds like the mill owner
Shouting, angry, and loud
I am glad he is not shouting at me.

Alexander Wood (10)
St Margaret's CE Primary School, Leeds

Boxing

Five good fast hooks
He's gone for the good win
He's going down, rapidly fast
Knock Out!

Wayne Sandham (10)
St Margaret's CE Primary School, Leeds

A Night-Time Tale

As I lay in bed at night,
I hear two cats begin to fight.
Their yowling carries on and on,
Until it seems that one has won.
But just as I'm drifting off to sleep,
A little cat begins to weep.
So climbing slowly out of bed,
I slip on my slippers and clutch my Ted.
And padding over to the window sill,
I pull back the curtain and sit really still.
The tabby, it hisses and arches its back,
But the poor little black one just doesn't have the knack.
I can stand it no longer, so creep down the stairs,
I'll get into trouble, but nobody cares.
The front door creaks open, I peep round the door,
Am I ready to do this? I'm not really sure.
But once I'm outside and crossing the lawn,
My tiredness takes over, I let out a yawn.
I think I must look quite a scary sight,
With slippers and Ted, (not equipped for the night!)
Because the tabby decides it's the end of the war,
So I pick up the black cat and bring him indoors.
Snuggled in bed, safe from his foe,
The little black cat curls up on my toes.

Lois Brown (11)
St Margaret's CE Primary School, Leeds

Cat Attack

Prowling slyly with a malevolent grin,
A jet-black shine on its fur, on its skin,
The cat, now determined but its prey stays stiff
Triumphant she remains now approaching the cliff.

Following her wherever she goes,
The cat needs to eat, its hunger grows,
On top of the mountains her heart sinks,
Into the snow where the frosty wind blinks.

The girl now knows there's nothing she can do,
The bloodthirsty cat knows this too,
Creeping slowly, she knows the cat will prevail,
All she can think of is its long curly tail.

The cat with no collar, no family, no home,
The cat with the hunger, the danger, all on its own,
No one will pet it, feed it or try,
They don't understand or hear the cat's cry.

Jessica Womack (10)
St Margaret's CE Primary School, Leeds

Anger

Anger is red like the raw
Steak I ate.

Anger tastes like the cold
Cabbage in the fridge.

Anger smells like the sweaty
Gym socks, put in my drawer.

Anger looks like the sky
On an unlit day.

Anger sounds like the
Horrible sound of my violin.

Anger feels like the blood
Draining from my skin.

Kieran Olsen (10)
St Margaret's CE Primary School, Leeds

Match Of The Waves

The blue waves are
Smashing against the
Red wall and then the
Sub comes on
And the wall
Breaks and the
Sea rocks a
Celebration but
Still it's only
My imagination
As I look
Through my
Window
On the
Rainiest
Day
Ever.

Nathaniel Warnes (10)
St Margaret's CE Primary School, Leeds

Rabbits

R abbits are cuddly and sweet
A lways bubbly and jump about
B ut they can bite you
B ut you still love it
I n the garden they hide
T hey hop out at you
S o they are lots of fun.

Toni-Louise Stanley (10)
St Margaret's CE Primary School, Leeds

My Fear

My fear is a
Very dull brown.

My fear tastes
Like my boiling
Blood.

My fear smells
Like the stench
Of my burning
Flesh.

My fear looks like
A big huge monster.

My fear sounds
Like my yelling
In pain.

My fear feels
Like my fear itself
Haunting me every day.

Joshua Malone (9)
St Margaret's CE Primary School, Leeds

Cat

Cats are great
Soft like feathers
Warm and cosy
Like a baby's blanket
Gentle as a teardrop
Sleeping like a baby
Happy as a child at Christmas.

Aimee McKellar (10)
St Margaret's CE Primary School, Leeds

Winner

My emotion is blue and yellow

My emotion tastes like a warm Bovril
At half-time in the cold wet weather.

My emotion smells like the horrible
Smelling toilets in the stadium.

My emotion smells like my idol
Barry McDermott scoring the winning try.

My emotion sounds like the commentator
Saying Rhinos have won 100 to 75 to Bulls.

My emotion feels like us winning the challenge cup.

We are the winners!

Thomas Harris (10)
St Margaret's CE Primary School, Leeds

Happiness In The Sun

Happiness is yellow like the burning sun
Happiness tastes like sweet strawberries
Happiness smells like scented candles around your bath
Happiness looks like a field of roses in the heat,
Happiness sounds like gentle music,
Happiness feels like someone massaging you.

Pollyanna Yeadon (10)
St Margaret's CE Primary School, Leeds

Chelsea

C hampions of the premiership
H eroes one and all
E verlasting companionship
L iving strong and tall
S torming high above the rest
E ager to take on any one
A rsenal are their biggest test

A pplause, skills - a fantastic run
F ootball they are the best
C helsea have won.

Andrew Edser (10)
St Margaret's CE Primary School, Leeds

Happiness

Happiness is yellow like the sunshine
It tastes like melting chocolate
It smells like pears
It looks like best friends
It sounds like laughing
It feels like joy.

Rosie Woodgate (10)
St Margaret's CE Primary School, Leeds

At My Birthday Party

At my birthday party
We had little sausages
But the cats took them.

At my birthday party
We had lots of jelly
But my guinea pig sat on it.

At my birthday party
We had loads of cheese
But my mouse ate it.

At my birthday party
We had a massive cake
But we ate that.

Dominic Fogden (10)
St Margaret's CE Primary School, Leeds

Who Is De Pony?

Who is de pony dat kicks de saddle
Then jumps for it over de fence?

Storm is a pony so full of zest
Storm is de pony dat just can't rest.

Who is de pony dat set de pace
Where mares and colts dem start to race?

Storm is a pony so full of zest
Storm is a pony dat just can't rest.

Who is de pony dat laze around
After mares and colts dem start to race?

Storm is a pony so full o' zest
Storm is a pony dat just can't rest.

Jade Corbridge (10)
St Matthias' CE Primary School, Leeds

Wings

If I had wings . . .
I would skim over the pale blue sea like ink splodges on the paper
And swim with the dolphins.

If I had wings. . .
I would fly to Blackpool
And swim on the beach
And sunbathe on the glittery yellow sun.

If I had wings . . .
I would fly over Yorkshire and see the beautiful flowers like paint
Dots on a green sheet of paper.

If I had wings . . .
I would fly as high as an eagle and race it down the sharp
                                        mountainside.

Misbah Zahir (9)
St Matthias' CE Primary School, Leeds

Wings

If I had wings . . .
I would fly over the rooftop
Like a pearly white beautiful dove.

If I had wings . . .
I would play in the sky
Swerving right and left
Like an exotic swallow.

If I had wings . . .
I would sleep on a cloud of peace
And throw all my problems away.

If I had wings . . .
I would meet Doctor Who
And be taken from future to past.

Emma Terrell (10)
St Matthias' CE Primary School, Leeds

Wings

If I had wings . . .
I would jump with dolphins
Across the vast seas.

If I had wings . . .
I would fly swiftly
Through the fluffy clouds.

If I had wings . . .
I would eat a chunk of the moon
As tasty as a cookie.

If I had wings . . .
I would listen to the bolting wind
In mid-air and rush through the air.

Eamon Droko (10)
St Matthias' CE Primary School, Leeds

Wings

If I had wings . . .
I would
Skim the beautiful seas,
Racing the heroic fish.

If I had wings . . .
I'd fly past Mars,
Touching the rock as I speed past.

If I had wings . . .
I'd fly over a horrific tornado
Feeling the rippling sides.

If I had wings . . .
I'd fly to the top of the biggest building in the world,
Listening to the beauty of the birds' song.

Reece George (9)
St Matthias' CE Primary School, Leeds

Celebrity

1, 2, 3, a girl like me
can never be a
celebrity. I hope and pray that one day
a chance will
come my way.

I do what I have to do
to survive and hope that God forgives me.
I need a friend to help me mend the errors of my way.

People stare
they just don't care
how much it
hurts me.

It will be my turn to shine and show them what I am made of
but until that day, I did the crime so I will serve my time.

Shannon Wharton (9)
St Thomas More RC Primary School, Sheffield

Poem

(Continued from the opening verse written by Brian Patten)

When we opened the door yesterday
Beyond it we found
Something unique and fabulous
That left us spellbound.

Then we looked around and
We found a little spark lying on the ground.

When we said, 'Hi,' the spark started to cry,
We asked him, 'Why?'
The little spark answered,
'You've woken me up from my beauty sleep.'

'I'm glad we've woken you up
You are beautiful enough.'

Alex Barker (11)
St Thomas More RC Primary School, Sheffield

Tommy The Tom Cat

Tommy the tom cat
Is a very fat cat
He's out and about
He's on the run
Always looking for some fun.
He's prancing and dancing
All about
And he's very heavy and
Full of trout.
He's always having accidents
Falling out of trees
His nine lives now
Are down to only three.
He hides in bushes, he hides in sheds,
Waiting for birds and mice to turn their heads.
He waits and waits till the time is just right
But he seems to be better
Catching them at night.
The winter is on its way now
And the weather's getting cold.
Tommy likes to stay in more now he's getting old.
His fur is going grey and his eyesight's getting poor
But his old lady owner just loves him more and more.

Chloe Ingram (9)
St Thomas More RC Primary School, Sheffield

All About Me

Now I'm nine
I stop and think
What it was like
When I was eight.
First I was fine,
Then I had pain in my tummy
I cried for my mummy
So she took me to the doctor
Who sent me to the hospital, quick
So I was seen to in a tick
At first I was scared of needles
But now I've had it done
I'm all prepared for
What's to come
I had an investigation
It only seemed like two seconds
But it was really two hours
When I came back I didn't know
Where I was
I hope I'm not in again
It really hurts when I'm in pain
So let's hope when I'm ten
I'm a lot better again.

Ruby Doane (9)
St Thomas More RC Primary School, Sheffield

Best Friends Stick Together

Best friends stick together through thick and thin
We stick together through the rough and the tough.
We have tears, we have laughter,
When I go to the park they're always in my heart.
We go to swim in the sea, to see what we can see.
We love to go to the zoo, to see what we can do.
We like to go on holiday, best of all with friends.
When we're all at school we all feel ever so cool.
We all help each other without any doubt
Because we're all best friends and best friends stick
Together forever.
When we're apart it breaks our hearts
So we're together forever and ever
Because we are all the bestest of friends forever and ever and ever.

Kimberley Revill (9)
St Thomas More RC Primary School, Sheffield

Should I Go?

It's two o'clock on Saturday
Should I go and watch them play?
I put on my football shirt, the one that's lucky,
Oh no! I didn't put in the wash and it's all mucky.
I walk to the ground with the rest of the crowd,
Everyone shouting, the noise is so loud.
I enter the ground and take my seat,
Will it be a win or a defeat?
It's 4.45 and the game is over,
I should have fetched my four leaf clover.
It happens every week, I should have known,
Next week I will stay at home all alone.

William Hodkin (9)
St Thomas More RC Primary School, Sheffield

The Seashore

On a breezy but warm day
There lay the beach
With the coloured shells and green slimy seaweed and the
Cosy warm sand
And the sea is just sparkling blue
With the crabs and the small fish
And the sea and rocks and stones are all in a dish
There are sounds of the people having fun
And the waves are making a big loud drum
The sand is soft, warm and is nice to walk on and feel
The colour is goldy and it makes you feel real
There are sounds of the birds humming in the sky
And it makes you want to fly
And the sound of the wind flowing slowly through you as go by
And it really makes you want to cry
You find in the sky lots of birds humming
Trees flowing
And wind blowing
You will find bright blue clouds drifting all around
And they reflect on the ground
The beach is in Skegness
And there are approximately 1000 people who go there.

Bronia Johnston (8)
St Thomas More RC Primary School, Sheffield

William-Man

Last week I was in trouble
In trouble pretty deep
My mum and dad were yelling
I moved quickly on my feet.

My dad found me under my bed
He asked me if I was out of my head
Why he asked in despair
Had I cut my brother's hair?

'Mum said he needed a trim,'
I tried to explain to him
'A trim!' he yelled, going red
'He's no hair left, now get to bed.'

'I was only trying to help,' I said
But Dad said, 'Get to bed.'
Even though I was in trouble
I knew it was going to be double
As soon as Mum went in the porch to get her hat
And saw the state of Henry the cat.

William Matthews (9)
St Thomas More RC Primary School, Sheffield

Zoo Animals

If you go to the zoo
There are some things you could do
See the sea lions catch their fish
See the snakes wiggle and hiss
See the monkeys swing through trees
When you only come up to a giraffe's knees
See the elephants swing their trunks
They use it to eat and dunk
See the penguins wobble and play
They only know what they say.

Rebecca Monfredi (9)
St Thomas More RC Primary School, Sheffield

Summer

Flowers bloom, weather's hot, everybody's happy
Birds are singing and bees are humming,
The farmer's collecting his crop.
Mum and Dad are gardening, cutting grass
And trimming the hedge.
Dad listening to the cricket score to see if Yorkshire's won.
We're in the paddling pool trying to cool down,
It's really hot this summer,
We'll probably go brown
We're going on our holidays to somewhere very nice,
We're going for two weeks, hip, hip, hooray.
I love summer for all that it brings like ice cream, trips out,
Late nights and sun and sand.
But I like summer because we have such fun,
We play and play and play,
The only dread I have now is that school returns five weeks
                                                    from today.

Matthew Carter (10)
St Thomas More RC Primary School, Sheffield

Untitled

My dad's got a car
It won't go far.

My mum laughs
Her's goes fast.

My dad's is blue
The same as my shoe.

My mum's is red
She likes to go to bed.

Emmi wants a pink one
I hope she gets one.

Jordan wants a fast one
So he isn't the last one.

Ethan Barton (9)
St Thomas More RC Primary School, Sheffield

The Reluctant Poet

They told me to write a poem,
It didn't have to rhyme,
But it kept coming back to me, line after line.
I'm trying my best not to speak in verse,
But the rhyming just gets worse and worse!
I'll go away and try to think
While washing some dishes at the kitchen sink.
All my efforts are in vain,
All this pressure hurts my brain.
I'm getting tired and I'll put down my pen,
I'll have a bath and try again.
Now I'm back and squeaky clean,
I think my teachers are being quite mean.
Twenty lines long it has to be,
What do these people want out of me?
Right, here I go, just one more try,
If I rhyme once more, I'll crack up and cry.
There I go again, I've lost my cool
I guess I'm just a poetic fool.
Right that's it, I give in,
Anyone want a biscuit?

Chloe Start (10)
St Thomas More RC Primary School, Sheffield

When We Opened The Door . . .

(Continued from the opening verse written by Brian Patten)

When we opened the door yesterday
Beyond it we found
Something unique and fabulous
That left us spellbound.

We both looked around
And we glanced at the ground
Hearing a mystical sound.

As I looked at the crumbling ground
Up came a sparkle to my eye,
And the little sound said, 'Hello.'
And we said, 'Hi.'

The sparkle was blue
As we said, 'Who are you?'
A little elf peeked out
And it gave a little shout.

'Could you please give me some help,
I've gone the wrong way
I want to get back to yesterday.'

We closed our eyes
And chanted a spell
Something as unique and fabulous
With us couldn't dwell.

When we opened the door yesterday
We knew we had found
An elf so unique and fabulous
Forever spellbound.

Michaela Revill (11)
St Thomas More RC Primary School, Sheffield

Untitled

(Continued from the opening verse written by Brian Patten)

When we opened the door yesterday
Beyond it we found
Something unique and fabulous
That left me spellbound.

Then we heard a sound
That made our hearts pound
We saw a sparkle of blue
Then appeared a little shoe.

The shoe jumped up and down
We followed it all the way round
The shoe led us to a house where no one lived.

We looked outside
It was bare, we waited a while
Guess what was there?
Blue sparkles everywhere.

The spell was broken
We closed the door
The sparkles of blue
Forever true, when we found
Something unique and fabulous
That left us spellbound.

Eleanor Gott (10)
St Thomas More RC Primary School, Sheffield

Untitled

(Continued from the opening verse written by Brian Patten)

When we opened the door to yesterday
Beyond it we found
Something unique and fabulous
That left us spellbound.

That makes a small sound
That is how we found
The mysterious thing
That left me spellbound.

Then suddenly out of the blare
A magical spark came out of the air
It must be something dangerous or good
That led me to a deep dark wood.

It made me full of happiness
Just like it should
There was a voice from nowhere
Mumbling by
Then it said, 'Hi.'

That was the end of me
So I can say it didn't go just like that
I am trapped in spellbound land
(But really I'm daydreaming in no-man's-land in class!)

Emma Townsend (11)
St Thomas More RC Primary School, Sheffield

Untitled

(Continued from the opening verse written by Brian Patten)

When we opened the door yesterday
Beyond it we found
Something unique and fabulous
That left us spellbound.

When we opened the door yesterday
We heard something in the sparkly ground
Me and my friend heard a mysterious sound
Then something started spinning around.

When we opened the door yesterday
There were all different things, then something poked out
Which started to cry
We didn't ask why.

When we opened the door yesterday
We heard another sound
So me and my friend looked back at the sparkling ground
Then some coloured dust spun around.

When we opened the door yesterday
We locked that door that day
And never opened it again
But it still left us spellbound.

Ella Jeffcock (10)
St Thomas More RC Primary School, Sheffield

Space Adventure

(Continued from the opening verse written by Brian Patten)

When we opened the door yesterday
Beyond it we found
Something unique and fabulous
That left us spellbound.

A door opened and we went into space
I never knew that our solar system,
Was such a stupendous place.

I've heard rumours that a man fell down a crater,
But the good news is,
He appeared three days later!

Next we went to Saturn
Where we saw something unbelievable
Space is really unliveable.

We can't stay here forever
It's getting sort of cold
I can't be up here for goodness sake; I'm only ten years old!

Look over there
Oh, wow a comet
No, behind it
An abandoned rocket.

We got onboard and returned to the ground
We've see things so unique and fabulous
We've been really spellbound!

Russell Marsden (10)
St Thomas More RC Primary School, Sheffield

The Dog

The dog, man's best friend,
If you break, he will help you mend,
He will always be your best friend
And his legs can bend.

His eyes are blue,
He likes to chew.
He doesn't go, *Moo,*
You can help him choose what to do.

His muscles are tough,
He can play rough.
He likes to drink Duff,
And still he is tough.

He likes to eat,
Just give him some meat.
He will stay neat,
Just don't give him a beat.

The dog, man's best friend,
If you break, he will help you mend,
He will always be your best friend,
And his legs can bend.

Thomas Needham (9)
St Thomas More RC Primary School, Sheffield

Untitled

(Continued from the opening verse written by Brian Patten)

When we opened the door yesterday
Beyond it we found
Something unique and fabulous
That left us spellbound.

Then we opened a door
Into another dimension
All different colours
When we opened the door yesterday.

It was something different
Like yesterday wasn't meant to be
A tiny creature we had to set free.

The door was unlocked
We opened the door
The creature ran out in a flash
When we opened the door yesterday.

The creature thanked us
For saving him
The spell was wearing thin
We had to return to our original world
When we opened the door to yesterday.

Malcolm Smith (11)
St Thomas More RC Primary School, Sheffield

My Fat Cat

My fat cat is totally black,
My fat cat has a silver hat,
My fat cat has a friendly rat,
My fat cat lives on a mat.

My fat cat speaks in a secret code,
My fat cat lives at 4 St Margaret's Road
My fat cat lives with me, my mum and dad,
My fat cat is really mad.

My fat cat has a mum that's really dumb,
My fat cat has a dad that's very bad,
My fat cat has a mate that's a parrot
That chews on an old carrot.

My fat cat can bake a pie
My fat cat can tell a lie
My fat cat can make a cake
My fat cat can make mistakes.

My fat cat is my best friend!

Rachael Bradley (10)
St Thomas More RC Primary School, Sheffield

My Yamoto Team

Yamoto team is the best of the best
It zooms and zooms
And sounds like the best.

The engine's small and it looks like a ball
And it crashed into the wall.

I rub and polish to make it shine
It gleams and shines in the sunshine
Look at the gleam on this bike of mine.

All ready to go riding now
On the road on the mucky line
The dust flies high, as I whizz by.

Thomas Smith (9)
St Thomas More RC Primary School, Sheffield

Henry VIII

Henry VIII had six good wives
He never cared of their lives
His life was so glum,
The girls were so dumb.
Henry VIII was so, so small
All his wives were very tall.
Anne of Cleves and Catherine Parr
Neither of them got very far.
One lost her home,
The other lost her head,
Just as Henry always said.

In the castle they liked to eat and drink
The women wore big long dresses and lots of mink
A jester came to make them laugh
When he failed he felt their wrath
To the dungeon he did go,
Left out in the rain and snow
Lady Jane was the last,
Just because they had a past.
Henry was very fat
They never used to have a mat
But then their life ended
Then nobody got defended.

Catherine Monfredi (9)
St Thomas More RC Primary School, Sheffield

My Cat Happy

My cat Happy gave me such a fright
As I opened the back door she ran into the night
I shouted and shouted for her to come back home
Oh Happy, don't leave me waiting here alone

I locked the door and went to bed
'Don't worry, Caitlin,' my mum said
And sure enough in the morning
There was my Happy loudly snoring.

Caitlin Ryan (8)
St Thomas More RC Primary School, Sheffield

My Little Puppy Molly

Her coat is black,
With shiny little sparkles.
Her nose is wet,
Her tail wags a lot,
She has long dangly ears,
That are full of curls,
With dark shiny eyes
And lashes that twirl.

She makes a barking sound
When she's dashing around
And she makes me laugh
When she acts like a clown,
She even makes me giggle,
When I'm feeling down.

I love my little puppy
Sometimes she can be bad
But she is a little sweetie
And so much fun to have.

Bradley Phillips (9)
St Thomas More RC Primary School, Sheffield

Bath Time

In goes the water,
Not too hot,
Squeeze out the bubble stuff,
In goes the lot.

In goes my whale
In goes my boat
In goes all the toys
That I can float.

Now my bath is ready
What else can there be
I think I can remember . . .
In goes *me.*

Karis Dykes (9)
St Thomas More RC Primary School, Sheffield

I'm Too Cool For School!

School, school is so boring,
School is the most boring thing.
School, school, I'm too cool,
School, school doesn't rule.
School, school I need tools
To break out of school.

Lessons, lessons are so boring,
Lessons are the most boring thing.
Lessons, lessons I'm too cool,
Lessons, lessons don't rule.
Lessons, lessons I need tools
To break out of boring lessons.

Teachers, teachers are so boring,
Teachers are the most boring thing.
Teachers, teachers, I'm too cool,
Teachers, teachers, think they rule.
Teachers, teachers I need tools
To break out of boring *school!*

Rebecca Bradley (10)
St Thomas More RC Primary School, Sheffield

Dogs

Dogs have a special thing
Dogs sing, dogs dance
Dogs jump up, dogs prance
Dogs make people laugh
Dogs have to charge to jump up on a trampoline
And bounce so high up into the sky
Too much excitement dogs just fall asleep in the sky.

Esme Hazelby (10)
St Thomas More RC Primary School, Sheffield

The Journey To The Seaside

We are all loading up the car
Seaside we're going, *yes* we are.
I wanted to take my great big bear
But Mum said 'No' it's *sooooo* unfair.

I banged my head getting in the car
And then asked Dad if we're going far
He started up the engine
Brum, brum, brum
Then I saw the sandwiches
Yum, yum, yum.

We drove to the bottom of the street
And then I asked Mum for a sweet
She said, 'No,' and I said, 'Why?'
And she gave me a great big *sighhhhh!*

She shouted at me
And I said it's not fair
So I shouted really loud
And we argued all the way there.

We went down this *big, big* hill
That was very steep
Then this car went in front of us and Dad went
Beep, beep, beep.

Jade Evans (10)
Snaith CP School

The Elephant And The Mouse

A mouse met an elephant
The mouse whispered,
'What big feet has thee, has thee,
What big feet has thee.'
'Aye,' trumpeted the elephant,
And went on his way, his way,
And went on his way.

Harry Agar (11)
Snaith CP School

A Journey To The Sea

Here we go
Once again
Loading me up
My back's in pain.

Chug, chug
Faster and faster
Next thing we know
There's a *disaster!*

Now we've got a
Tyre flat
The engine hissing
Oh no, not that!

Now it's all repaired
And well
The engine's running
The car's swell.

Now we are
Nearly there
In a field
We see a bear.

Now we'd better
Slow right down
In half a mile
We reach the town.

Now we'd better
Park the car
There's a space
Not very far.

Josh Breeden (9)
Snaith CP School

A Bad Day

Soon as I get up
I bang my foot
Get bitten by the dog
That stupid mut!

Make the bed
PS2's bust
Find my Game Boy
Covered in dust!

Milk's gone off
Have to have toast
Set off to my mates
Walk into a lamp post!

Go back home
Mum's gone to the shop
Go for a drink
There's no pop!

Fancy a sing?
How about karaoke?
La, la, la
Oh my voice is all croaky.

Eating a Mars bar
Waving a tick
Bllaaaaagh!
I've been sick.

Oh at last
End of the day
Three words,
Hip hip hooray!

Jack Taylor (9)
Snaith CP School

The Journey To The Sea

Ooh I love
Going to the seaside
It is so much fun
Brummm brummm
Here I come
Packing the car
Is so not fun
Oh no the car won't start
Chug, chug, brummm, brummm
The car sets off
And here I come
Oh Dad you're going too fast
The speed camera has just flashed
I have just seen Gran
Passing by
Why, oh why?

Holly Price (9)
Snaith CP School

Make-Believe

In my land of make-believe
Sun, seas and honeybees,
Red, yellow and orange trees,
Boats, moats and goats,
Am I dreaming?
The sun is gleaming
Oh it's all in my head
I best go to bed
Goodnight my land of make-believe.

Chloe Smith (10)
Snaith CP School

A Journey To The Sea

Brrrruuuummm
Come along this
Path every year
Can't wait till we
Get to the pier.

Getting faster
Zzzooooooming along
The engine *boooooming*
Carrying a big load today.

Nearly there
Down the hill
'I don't feel very well,' says Phil
Now I better slow down.

Finally we are there
That wasn't that bad
Dad took a sigh he's glad
Hiiiiissssss went the car.

Now we're nearly
Home sweet home
I can't wait
Till I get washed with foam.

Charley Britton (9)
Snaith CP School

Half Cat, Half Monster

Half cat, half monster, that is me
With two wibbly wobbly eyes to help me see
All day I hide up in a tree
Watch out case I pounce
How very scary!

Elizabeth Holroyd (11)
Snaith CP School

Sweets

Galaxy, Yorkie
Lion Bar, Dream,
Mars bar, Gobstoppers,
Jelly beans.

Snickers, Smarties,
After Eights, Crunchy
Cola bottles,
Cream Eggs, Munchies.

Black Jack, Werthers,
Minstrels, Kit-Kat
Topic, jaw breaks,
Haribo, Tic-Tac.

Bubblegum, Twirl,
Time Out, Twix,
Now visit
The dentist.

Kevin Moles (10)
Snaith CP School

Gold

Slowly, silently now the sun,
Beams down his golden fun.
He peers down through the trees,
And sees shadows of wasps
And shadows of bees.
Across the city he creeps,
And sees a hot boy who
Starts to weep.
He travels onto the town,
And sees the Queen wearing a crown.

James McKiernan (9)
Snaith CP School

Journey To The Sea

Gosh
How much stuff do they need
Food, juice
And a book to read.

Starting the engine
Gauge going up fast
Catching up speed
Beep, beep, sound a blast.

Going through tunnels
And up hills
Round bends
And my head kills.

Going slowly
Into town
We're nearly there
Dad's got a frown.

Here's a car park
Let's find a space
Lots of traffic
Going at a slow pace.

Not many spaces
For our car
Dad watch out!
There's some wet tar.

We're out of the car
The sun's not so bright
I think there was too much traffic
Cos now it's nearly night!

Sarah Dick (9)
Snaith CP School

My Sister

My mum's just had a baby
She's really, really sweet
She was born on firework night
Now that was a treat.

She has loads of toys
More than I ever had
And when she smiles at me
I'm really, really glad.

Her name is Finola
It's an unusual name
And everyone crowds around her
Like she's fame.

And when she goes to bed
I never want to let go
She's nice, warm and cuddly
Well you can't say no.

Molly Roper (10)
Snaith CP School

Sweets

Starburst, chocolate,
Kit-Kat, Rolo
Mars bar, Minty,
Bounty, Polo.

Skittles, Caramac,
Strawberry Cream
Jelly Babies,
Chocolate Dream.

I think I better stop
Right now
Because I feel sick,
But by the way
What a good pick.

Georgia Thompson (9)
Snaith CP School

Friends Or Sisters

I have a lot of friends
Some from Fair Oak
And some from Snaith,
But there is something more important
To me than friends
That's sisters!

Sisters are smart and special
They're the sprinkles on top of an ice cream
They're shining like the night stars
They're as bright as the morning sun!

They're always there
For younger brothers and sisters
They protect you from bullies
They'll cheer you up
When you feel sad
Yes, sisters will always be there for you!

Katie Oliver (11)
Snaith CP School

The Sun

Slowly, silently the sunlight
Shines in the morning, very bright
When I get up, it's time to go out!
If I open the door they start to shout
I'm the sun, bright and bold
I shine on everyone and I'm *gold!*

Gabi Wright (9)
Snaith CP School

Gold

Brightly burning now the sun,
Beams down like a golden bun.
All day long he peers and sees,
Golden fruit upon golden trees.
Every day he sees the birds,
But he cannot speak their words.
All the puddles after the rain,
Dry up in the sunny lane.
All the children playing out,
Are having chats all about
The sun!

Joe Ford (9)
Snaith CP School

Gold

When it's morning the sun comes out,
He shines so bright and does not shout.
The sun makes a lovely warm light,
But he goes back down at the start of night.
He sees shadows lots and lots,
And flowers in big plant pots.
The sun has no friends, none at all
Not even stars who are very small.

Robyn Bligh (9)
Snaith CP School

Gold

Slowly, silently now the sun
Looks down on a world of fun.
While he gives people a tan
Other people get out their fan.
One sunny day the doorbell rings
But the wasp gives people terrible stings.
Suddenly the sun gets brighter
And the world gets lighter.
He peeps through the window
Making the people's shadow.
The sun stretches out his rays
That makes it hot most of the days.
When it rains and makes rivers flow
The sun comes out and makes a rainbow.
After the hard long day
The hot sun sails away.

Lewis Kellett (10)
Snaith CP School

Gold

The sun burns hot in the day.
During a day in the month of May.
Then he sees a golden leech
On a very lonely beach.
He sees the children running round
And their shadows on the ground.
He goes round and gives a frown
Then he sees a baby hound.
The sun gets very bold,
And the sun is like gold.

Aaron Oxley (10)
Snaith CP School

Gold

The sun is gold,
It's never cold.

The sun is bright,
Until it's night.

It leaves shadows on the ground,
But does not make a sound.

The sun shines rays,
On sunny days.

The day is bright,
Oh what a sight.

The moon has come,
The sun is done.

Amy Oglesby (10)
Snaith CP School

Gold

The sun is bright.
He gives us all light.
He walks around
Without touching
The ground.
He gleams gold.
He is very blond.
Every day he watches
The children play.
Now sunset is here
The sun gives a cheer
Now he can rest so
The next day he can
Look his best.

Evie Childs (10)
Snaith CP School

Black Magic

Stalking through the jungle
Searching for her prey.
Give it to her cubs
Every night and day.
If a human comes her way
She will give him one
And make him stay.

You will find me in the zoo
And in the jungle too.
If you wonder who
I am, here's a clue
I'm a big black cat
And at night I look blue.

Stephanie Wigg (9)
Snaith CP School

Gold

Slowly, silently, the sun gleams
With his bright light beams.

It goes down when it's night
Waits till it's light and plays
With his kite.

Now it's morning the sun comes out
To see lots of children
Playing about.

Every morning the sun shines
Bright
Shines through the trees when it's light.

Naomi Sweetman (9)
Snaith CP School

The Abandoned Dog

As I walk to school I notice an abandoned house,
I look through the windows
And see a face staring miserably at me,
My friends call me but I stay staring,
Staring at the window smiling.

His fur is white, fluffy and soft,
He wags his tail
As if to say,

'Be my owner now.'
I can't help it, he's helpless.

It happens the next day and next,
But now I look in the window, no sad face.
Instead I see the face
Standing next to me,
Our wish came true, he's my dog now.

Izzy Procter (8)
Snaith CP School

The Haunted Window

Climb through the haunted window
Maybe goblins are out there
No one knows what could happen.

Climb through the haunted window
Maybe beanstalk and giants could be there.
Golden eagle or a big monster
Who knows what could be there.

Climb through the haunted window
Maybe a fierce dragon
The fire breathing type
So climb through the window

At least
I'm dreaming.

Sophia Christou (9)
Snaith CP School

Imagine

(Dedicated to Mr Derek Allen - headmaster and friend who recently died suddenly and is greatly missed by everyone at Snaith CP School)

There would be solid water dying by slaughter
Children having paddys
Shouting at their daddies
Moats are . . .
Eating sailor's boats
And most hilarious is . . .
The toast ghosts
Eating my toast
So I will boast
In the morning I had a mountain of ironing
I didn't do it 'cause it was too tiring.

Steven Fearnley (10)
Snaith CP School

Different Colours

Blue as a shoe
Sparkling bright,
Pink makes you
Wink all through
The night,
Orange is a colour
Orange is a fruit
You can hear
The birds go
Tute! Tute!

Madeline Gallagher (8)
Snaith CP School

Red Nose Day

Red noses?
Red hair?
Red faces?
Red everywhere?

Wow, this is funny!
This isn't very fun!
I like this the best!
This costs too much?
I have nearly finished the game!
I am going to win!
Can I have another go?
What, I lost?

Red noses?
Red hair?
Red faces?
Red everywhere?

Heather King (11)
Snaith CP School

Flowers

F luttering in the gentle breeze
L ovely bright colours show
O ver the days new buds will come
W hen summer comes most flowers show
E very day they show themselves
R adiant and beautiful
S cent so wonderful.

Katy Sharp (9)
Snaith CP School

My Cousin

My cousin,
She isn't much trouble,
Her name is Alice,
She wants to live in a palace,
Her family thinks she's crazy,
But certainly not lazy,
She loves dancing,
And she loves prancing,
She loves singing along to songs too!

She is always funny,
And she likes it when it's sunny,
I couldn't ask for a better cousin,
And she hardly gets into trouble,
She goes to my school,
And I think she's cool!
That's *Alice!*

Rebecca Knowles (11)
Snaith CP School

Climb Through The Magic Window

Maybe you will land on a bed, fit for a queen
Or a mole hill
Climb through the magic window
Maybe there's a tree full of fruit
Or not a grape in sight
A nice refreshing stream
Or a scorching hot desert
Or maybe we should stay here
At least we are warm.

Thomas Boddye (9)
Snaith CP School

The Keyhole

Look through the keyhole
Maybe there's a bird in some trees
Or ponies rolling in mud
And deer with rabbits.

Look through the keyhole
Maybe there's a magic city
Or gold and silver lakes,
Magic horses with wings
And talking birds.

Look through the keyhole
Maybe there's an evil wood
Or spiders, big ones,
Eyes glaring at you.

At least
You're still
Breathing.

Evie Whiteley (8)
Snaith CP School

Dolphins - Haikus

Dolphins in the sea;
Playing with friends on the waves,
Dive into the blue.

Dolphins in the sea;
They are so mysterious,
But special to me.

Dolphins in the sea;
Always being mischievous,
Enchanting to me!

Georgia Kees (9)
Snaith CP School

What Is Red?

Red is an Indian
And
A colour
Filled with
Goodness
Red
Is blood
That's
In you
Red
Is *fire!*
That
Makes
You warm.

Ryan Cotterill (8)
Snaith CP School

Lions

I like lions
They hunt their prey
All day
You can hear them roar and raah
From very very far.

The males have long manes
Sometimes they can't be tamed
They fight really well
But watch out or they'll bite.

Molly Thompson (9)
Snaith CP School

What Is Blue?

A river is blue
Sailing across the canal side.
Eyes are blue
They shine in the sunlight
Flowers are blue
Sprouting in the sun
Walls are blue
They decorate your bedroom with sparkles
Cars can be blue
With their loud engines.
T-shirts are blue
They keep you warm.
The hands on a clock can be blue
Tick! Tock! Tick! Tock!

Kristina Curtis (8)
Snaith CP School

Light Blue

Blue is an ocean,
Blue is a sky,
Blue is a river,
Blue is a school T-shirt,
My favourite colour is blue,
My toothbrush is blue,
My pen is blue,
My book is blue.

Aidan Kirsopp (8)
Snaith CP School

Chips

Chips, chips, different chips
Yellow chips
Square chips
Triangular chips
Circular chips
Chips that
Crunch!
Crunch!
Crunch!
Burnt chips
Chips with coleslaw
Chips with ketchup
Fish and chips
Yummy! Yum!
Yummy!
I like fish and chips
And bread
I like
Chips and beans
I like them all!

Macauley Thornton (8)
Snaith CP School

My Sister - Haiku

My sister's left me
Training to be a teacher
At Cambridge Uni.

Jonathan Crossley (11)
Snaith CP School

What Is Blue?

The sea is blue
The waves are blue
The sky is blue
Chairs are blue
Deep blue
Gloves are blue
Pencils are blue
Sharpeners are blue
Bobbles are blue
Earrings are blue
Boxes are blue
Bottles are blue
Curtains are blue
Doors are blue
Letters are blue
Shoes are blue
Frogs are blue
Puddles are blue
Splash, splash!

Rose Thornton (8)
Snaith CP School

What Is Blue?

Blue sky,
Floating in the air.

Bluebirds flying in the sky,
Tweeting their own little song.

Glittering blue seas,
With fish swimming all around.

Blue T-shirts
Smooth and soft.

How can we live without blue?

Charlotte Dudley (7)
Snaith CP School

What Is Blue?

A bin is blue,
Rubbish! Rubbish! Rubbish!
Pencils are blue,
They are for writing with.
A Leeds top is blue,
Something people wear.
Pens are blue,
Things for colouring.
Boxes are blue,
They are for storing things in.
Lids are blue,
They are for bottles.
Trousers are blue,
They are for wearing.
Cars are blue,
Brum! Brum! Brum!
Sharpeners are blue,
They are for sharpening pencils.
Paper is blue,
You can make things out of it.

Jack Wilson (8)
Snaith CP School

What Is White?

The moon is white
And round
The snow is white
And crusty
Clouds are white
Floating in the sky
A4 paper is white
And for writing on
Parts of an aeroplane
Flying in the air
Are white.

Callum Chapman (7)
Snaith CP School

Red

I know what's red.
A team like Man Utd.
Or maybe a different team.
I know what's red
Blood in people.
I know what's red.
Red chairs.
I know what's red.
Cars, lorries, bikes, motorbikes.
I know what's red,
Drawers, toothpaste, brushes,
I know what's red
Man Utd
Shirt!

Jake Howard (7)
Snaith CP School

Gold And Blue

Money is gold.
Tutankhamun is gold and blue.

Toothbrushes are blue
Toothpaste is blue.
The button is gold.

Rings are gold.
Treasure is gold.

Ancient treasure is gold.
Our class is golden.

Some old pennies are gold.
One pound coins are gold.

Michael King (7)
Snaith CP School

What Is Blue?

Sky is blue
Breezing all around
T-shirts are blue
Trying to keep you warm.

Candyfloss is blue
Really, really fluffy
Sea is blue
Hear the waves flow.

Paint is blue
Dribbling on the floor
Folders are blue
Helpful for sheets.

*That's all the
Things
About blue!*

Ben Roper (8)
Snaith CP School

What Is Blue?

The sea is blue
Splish! Splash!
Sky is blue
Cloudy too
School
T-shirts
Are blue.
A bin is
Blue.
Blueberries
Are blue.

Harry Walton (7)
Snaith CP School

What Is Blue?

The sky is blue
With clouds floating by.

Eyes are blue
For you to see.

Clothes are blue
Nice to wear.

Flowers are blue
Needing lots of water.

Water is blue
It couldn't be red.

Hair bobbles are blue
They keep your hair up.

Scissors are blue
To cut up your paper.

Pencils are blue
To write with.

Jodie Gilson (7)
Snaith CP School

What Is Red?

Roses are red
A beautiful flower
Pencil cases are red
Cars are red
Zooming fast
Sunset is red
Sleeping so soundly.

Megan Backhouse (7)
Snaith CP School

What Is Black?

It is black at night
When we all go to sleep
When the stars are very bright
Black is dark on white paper
Paper is what we write on or draw on
Black goes away in the sunlight
At midday
Pencil cases are black
What you put your pencils and colours in
Hair can be black
Some people have knots in their hair
Dark brown looks like black
When it is very dark
Some birds are black
Like crows, ravens and of course . . .
Blackbirds.

Luke Wilson (7)
Snaith CP School

What Is Gold?

Gold is a crown,
Shining bright.
Gold is an owl,
Flying through the night.

Gold is a brooch,
With golden edges,
Golden jubilee,
Through the ages.

Tutankhamun,
And a golden death mask.

That's what
Gold is!

Georgie Smith (8)
Snaith CP School

What Is Blue?

Blue is a colour
Light blue
Is like the sky!

Dark blue is like the
Sea!
Roaring at
You!
Material is blue
And so are you
Tutankhamun is blue
Blue as a shoe
Sparkling bright
At you
Blue is a shirt
A curtain is blue
As bright as you
Water is blue
And so are you.

Rachel Tate (7)
Snaith CP School

What Is Green?

Apples are green
Juicy and sweet

Grass is green
Little bugs in it

Leaves are green
Stems growing through it

Sometimes books are green
For you to read.

Bethany Knight (7)
Snaith CP School

What Is Red?

Ketchup is red
Squirt! Squirt!

Tomatoes are red
Slurp! Slurp!

Jam is red
Spread! Spread!

Pens are red
Scribble! Scribble!

Motorbikes are red
Vroommm! Vroommm!

Sean Younger (7)
Snaith CP School

Green

Grass is green
Trees are green
Flowers are green
Weeds are green
Green is sweet
Lovely to eat
Mouldy green
How can you live without green?

Holly Denby (7)
Snaith CP School

Amy's Cat

Ears like stuck up bits of paper
Teeth like arrows
Back like a sheet of felt
Nose like a tipped up triangle!
Tail like a long rope
Squeaks like a guinea pig
Yawns like a rat . . .
As short as a mouse
With whiskers like bits of string
It's Pebbles, my precious cat.

Amy Mackenzie (8)
Walkeringham Primary School

Merlin The Whippet

Ears like a pointed arrow,
Teeth like the beak of a sparrow,
Back like a bony old man,
Nose like a crumpled can.
A whimper, like squeaking old soap.
Smile like the beam of a sun,
Legs like a skinny bit of wire,
But so fast he can run!

Iona Murray (9)
Walkeringham Primary School

Football Game

Silence reigns over the green grass.
Whistle blows . . .
Thud! A blistering ball goes one to the other.
Clumps of grass fly from their designated spots.
Clangs from the goal mouth as the upright is hit.
Players fly to the well cut grass, after a hard tackle.
A sound of the wind being pushed down as the ref lifts
A yellow card.
The ball yells as it reaches blistering heights
When a free-kick is curled into the white chalked box.
The ball flies into the net, like a butterfly being caught.
Cheers go around as the final whistle blows.
Players start to shake hands and celebrate.
So movement ends . . .
For now.

Jack Rogers (11)
Walkeringham Primary School

Volcano

Soft, still, calm, quiet,
Shaking, shaking,
Rumbling, smoky,
Banging, booming,
Crashing!
Bang, bang, bang
Tumbling, rumbling,
Spitting, squirting,
Bubbling, smoky,
Rumbling, rumbling,
Slowly, calm,
Stopping, stopping,
Stopped!

Emma Frost (10)
Walkeringham Primary School

The Volcano

Bubbling
Bubbling
Boiling hot
Rising
Spitting, spraying
Firing
Shooting
Erupting
Burning
Exploding
Lava rushing down fast, faster
Suddenly
Calm
Silent
Stopping
Stopped
Burning
Burnt
Everything's
Burnt.

Zach Beard (9)
Walkeringham Primary School

Blue

The blue sky looks down at the blue sea,
Carefully swaying in the breeze
I can see baby blue eyes
A tiny bluebird egg
As fragile as China
I love blue silent nights.

Megan Pearcy (8)
Walkeringham Primary School

The Match In The Darkness

Quiet . . .
Silence . . .
Scraping sound fills the darkness
A small innocent flame starts to glow . . .
It gets brighter and brighter
Shouts in the dark
It swirls and twists,
The naked flame burns,
And catches!
The grey, black smoke rises rapidly,
The flame dies down
Slowly . . .
Silently . . .
. . . a rich charcoal aroma fills the
Darkness.

Jake Beard (11)
Walkeringham Primary School

Rabbit

Hopping,
Running,
Can't keep track of her,
Twisting,
Turning,
Can't keep track of her,
Bobbing,
Jumping,
Can't keep track of her,
She runs into the undergrowth,
Slowing down,
Walking,
Hiding in her burrow,
Away from harm's reach.

Beth Burley (10)
Walkeringham Primary School

Streams Are Golden

A shimmering stream in the light,
Wandering and weaving as a lost one does.
Trickles on and on,
Moved by a silent breeze . . .
Then
Down
Plummeting
Plunging
Spluttering
Spitting
Crushing
Cascading
Descending
Down . . .
Onto the rocks below,
Then
Dragged to the sleeping lake,
A drop sounds on the water
A ripple emerges . . .
Then silence . . .

Jack Bramham (11)
Walkeringham Primary School

Kelly

Ears like a grey sky
Teeth like shiny arrows
Nose like wet ping pong ball
Tail like a horse's mane
Claws like pointed diamonds
Back like a furry rug
Whiskers like chopped pieces of wire
And what is her name?

Kelly the rabbit of fame!

Katie-Ann Wickens (9)
Walkeringham Primary School

Grey And Black

Grey is a bone crushing wind,
Grey is a tornado ripping down a city in seconds
Until the ragging anger subsides,
Grey is a shiny sequinned tile standing still in glory,
Grey is an elephant sleeping silently
Snoozing as still as a statue
Grey is the night.

Black is the back of a great white shark,
Black is the computers,
Black is a traffic light box
Black is a greyhound
Black is a dusty wood.

Aaron Green (8)
Walkeringham Primary School

The Storm

The sea raged forward,
Roaring like an angry beast,
Erupting with anger and hate to all in its path,
Only to be fuelled by gale force winds of rage,
And aggressive lightning strikes,
Evil black clouds hang over,
Controlling everything and blocking the sun,
Until they give way to sunlight.

Nick Rodgers (11)
Walkeringham Primary School

The Moving Horse

Clip, clop, clip, clop
Going into a stop
Clip, clop, clip, clop
Speeding up a little bit more
Gallop, gallop, gallop
Charging like the puff coming out
Of a rhinoceros.

Rebecca Langley (9)
Walkeringham Primary School

Sports' Day

S weating with nervousness I stood there;
P eering at a sienna track
'O n your marks . . . get set . . . *Go!'* shrieked the judge:
R unning like a cheetah; I sprinted heart pounding.
T here in the distance was the pearl white finishing line:
S hining over it was a golden banner, dancing in the pale blue sky.

D own a hill I went nearly stumbling over in rapidity
A nd there was the pure white finishing line I hurdled over and . . .
Y es! I won the Sports' Day cup!

Bhagyashree Ganguly (9)
Wakefield Girls' High School Junior School

My Dog

Horrid smells,
Beautiful shells,
Metal bells,
My dog smells.
Slimy slugs,
Fleas on rugs,
Love and hugs,
My dog's got bugs.
Beautiful town,
People frown,
Laughing clowns,
My dog is brown.
Fluffy clouds,
Lovely and round,
Sweet and sound,
My dog is loud.
Pretty frocks,
Smelly socks,
Massive hawks,
My dog talks.
A cute lamb,
Red jam,
Pink, raw ham,
His name is Sam.

Hannah Slack (8)
Wakefield Girls' High School Junior School

Fireworks

Fiery Catherine wheels whizz and spin round,
Round and round the Catherine wheels go,
Catherine wheels are pretty.

In the pitch-black sky colours blaze, burning brightly.
Rockets zoom into the air.
Every single firework explodes in the moonlit sky.

Whizzing fireworks whizz round,
Oh, what a great sight!

The fireworks all have different noises,
They *Bang! Woosssssh! Scream!*

Samantha Lancaster (9)
Wakefield Girls' High School Junior School

Flowers

Blossom falling from the trees
Dancing in the cool breeze
Sunflowers have just been born
A farmer grows his yellow corn
Pansies are a dazzling sight
In the bright new morning light
Daisies on the golden hills
Prancing by the old stone mills
Tulips grow in woods and field
Underneath the trees that shield
What a pleasant sight to see
Oh how much it means to me.

Lorna Bowers (9)
Wakefield Girls' High School Junior School

Skiing

Skiing is a thrill
An icy wintry chill.

Your skis start to slide,
And your arms spread out wide
As you rush down the snow-flourished slope.

Your cheeks start to flush,
As you fly past a bush,
And your poles saunter slowly behind you.

Snow flies out the way,
As you carry on through the tiring day.

You are flying through a carpeted white wonderland,
Truly your parents can't understand
The joy which sieges through your arms and hands.

You let all your energy blaze,
As crimson becomes your face.

All the trees sway behind you,
And all the buildings look like igloos.

Down in the valley you can hear laughter,
And then very shortly after,
Silence slinks softly and sneakily over the snowy slopes.

India Copley (9)
Wakefield Girls' High School Junior School

The Snoozing Hamster

Snoozing, sleeping Hamtro,
My hamster sleeps all day,
Curled up and cosy in his bed,
At night he's out to play.

Once the moon is in the sky,
He shuffles from his sleep,
Stretching his tiny pink clawed paws,
Through his plastic cage I peep.

He spies a bowl heaped high with food,
Eagerly he scurries to taste what's there,
He gobbles and chomps as his pouches balloon,
There's enough food in his mouth for a week and spare.

Now time to de-pouch,
So it's off back to bed,
Back where he started,
Tired and well fed.

Katie Idle (8)
Wakefield Girls' High School Junior School

Under The Sea

I walk alone along the beach
The tide is now out of reach,
The moon is out shining bright
The waves lapping, catching the light.

The ships upon the horizon sail
I look out to see a big blue whale,
A fountain blowing from its head
Then it quickly dives down to the seabed.

The scum and seaweed swerve
And make patterns in the smooth sand,
And I make my way back
Up onto dry land.

Louise Belton (9)
Wakefield Girls' High School Junior School

My Pets

My puppy sits and yawns on the bed
While he waits impatiently to be fed.
He snuggles up and waits by the fire
In the morning he waits for his desire.

My cat plays with a pink ball
Sometimes he sits on the stairs in the hall
I put on my shawl when the wind blows
My cat goes.

My tiny mouse lives on the shelf
When I look for a book he's all by his self.
When the sun starts to set
The little mouse gets upset.

My little lamb gambles and plays
In the long lazy summer days.
My little lamb has three legs, white and one brown
People say she should wear a crown.

Olivia McGrath (9)
Wakefield Girls' High School Junior School

My Dog

My dog runs and leaps about
My dog plays on a roundabout
My dog loves to play about
Always when there's another dog out.

My dog likes to go out in the sun
When he plays about he has lots of fun
I throw him a ball he catches it
And runs round like crazy until he's told to sit.

Later at night we make sure he's well fed
Before he curls up on the settee and goes to bed
We love him to pieces and I'm glad to say
When I wake up in the morning he makes my day.

Hannah Foy (9)
Wakefield Girls' High School Junior School

Dogs

There are fat dogs,
Black dogs, white dogs
Tall dogs, short dogs
All different types of dogs.

Dogs are used for different jobs
There are guard dogs
Police dogs
Blind dogs

Dogs have different personalities
Fun dogs
Pretty dogs
Fierce dogs

All dogs are nice
Especially my dog!

Rebecca Morris (9)
Wakefield Girls' High School Junior School

Horses

I like horses
I really do
Their fur so soft
I really do
To see them prancing
In fields so green
Their long tails swing
Silhouetted in the moonlight
When their riders ride them
They go gallop, gallop
Quickly across the hill
Out of sight.

Rebecca Hick (9)
Wakefield Girls' High School Junior School

Brothers

In the morning when I awake,
My brother has sneaked in beside me.

At night-time when I am ready for bed,
My brother shakes his tired little head.

The best times are weekends,
When we run around and have fun.

The worst times are weekdays,
When he is grumpy, horrible and mean.

Brothers come in different sizes,
Some are fat and some are thin,
Some are big and some are small,
But my brother's the best of them all.

Rosie Allsopp   (9)
Wakefield Girls' High School Junior School

Traffic

Red means stop
Red and amber means stop
Green you may go
And stop when amber is on its own

Not too slow
And not too fast
Just try to keep
Within those tracks

Look for the crossing man
Look for the children
This is the time when extra care should be taken.

Elizabeth Ward (9)
Wakefield Girls' High School Junior School

Parrots

P arrots are just so annoying because they walk and talk.
A nd flap about their beautiful wings flying here, there and back.
R acing across our beautiful garden covered with wonderful flowers.
R apidly flapping their marvellous wings leaving a trail of feathers
behind them.
O utside the ground is multicoloured as the sun is coming down.
T he parrots leave our coloured garden, after they had
an excellent day.
S ometimes they are just so annoying; I just *can't* cope with it!

Mary Tadross (9)
Wakefield Girls' High School Junior School

Fireworks

F ireworks whirl they spin and twirl
I nto the misty air they hurl
R eally they are a fantastic sight
E ach one bursting into the night
W hile bonfires blaze and Guy Fawkes dies
O ut of the burning embers rise
R ed, orange and yellow flickers
K eep away or you'll singe your knickers!
S o you thought it was going to be a serious poem!

Rachel Sugarman (9)
Wakefield Girls' High School Junior School

Animals

Animals, animals all around, cows in the field,
Ducks in the pond and horses hooves thundering on the ground.
Bees, buzzing brightly in the sunshine.
Pigs tails curly as can be, dogs barking
And horses munching, happily.

Alexandra Selby (9)
Wakefield Girls' High School Junior School

Banana

Banana, banana
Banana, banana

You junior chiquita
So yellow and green.

Banana, banana
Banana, banana

You've been in the sun too long
So now you're a sultana
A sultana banana.

Banana, banana
Banana, banana

So long and bendy
If straight was in,
You'd be so not trendy.

Banana, banana
Banana, banana

If I was a banana
Life would be grim
As soon as you're born,
You're peeled of your skin.

Bananas, bananas
Bananas, bananas

Some soft, some hard
Some green, some yellow
Oh I wish
You wouldn't go off too quickly
In this lunchbag of mine.

Banana, banana.

Jack Hanlon (11)
Westways Primary School

Maybe

Last night while I lay sleeping here
Some 'Maybes' crawled inside my ear.
They danced and partied all night long,
And sang their same old 'Maybe' song.

Maybe I'll be dumb at school,
Maybe they've closed the swimming pool.
Maybe I'll grow a big bum,
Maybe I'll turn dumb.
Maybe I'll fail that test,
Maybe I'll grow purple hair on my chest.
Maybe I'll be the worst in class,
Maybe I'll break some special glass.
Maybe I'll lose my hair,
Maybe I'll let in a wild bear.
Maybe I'll let out a big sigh,
Maybe I'll get squished by a pie.
Maybe I'll get beaten up,
Maybe I'll squish my cup.
Maybe I'll get big and fat,
Maybe I'll be worse than that!
Maybe I'll have a heart attack,
Maybe I'll get taken away in a sack.
Maybe I'll never come home,
Maybe I'll turn into a gnome.

Everything seems swell and then . . .

The night-time 'Maybes' strike again!

Cara Bradshaw-King (9)
Westways Primary School

Getting Ready

OK we're ready to go,
Oh no where's Adday?
Yared, Desta, do you know?
She's in the toilet
Thank you Jack, here she comes now.
Now can we go?
Yes, OK
We're halfway up the hill and Kalabe has forgotten his lunch.
Back we go again.
We're just about to set off again and Yared has to rush back to
Get his coat.
Right, we are nearly there and I notice Jack's T-shirt,
What a state and Dixie you're still wearing your slippers.
Go back again, come on.

We're at school, right, head count, so
Jack, Dixie, Kalabe, Yared, Adday and . . .
Where's Desta?
Where is she? Everybody search.
Phew, here she is, you nearly gave me a heart attack.
Escape, phew, all at school now it's all for the teachers to handle.

Adday Heller (9)
Westways Primary School

At The Zoo

If you want to get married at Chester Zoo.
This is what we can offer you.
The monkeys will serve you fruit
The great big giraffe will marry you
He will make you say 'I Do'
Peter the penguin will give you a pear
But he likes to bring his pet bear.
Two charming elephants will be bridesmaids for you
A choir of birds will sing to you
A proud lion will be your best man in his best black boots
At the zoo, at the zoo, at Chester Zoo.

Amy Taylor (11)
Westways Primary School

Toys I Can't Play With

Tamagotchis
Overrun the school!
Yo-yos and
Skipping ropes
In the yard

Clothes for Barbies? Not today.
And lots of make-up? No way!
Neat and tidy hair; no time for play.

Till SATs have finished on Friday.

PE - no maths!
Literacy and science are gone.
As for SATs and keeping quiet . . . well
Yelling is much more fun!

What a lot of games to share,
If you can use imagination
Tests get in the way of play but we
Hope for happy endings.

Holly Bowman (11)
Westways Primary School

Things I Like

I like doing shows
At school
For the mummies and daddies.

I like the songs
And the actions.
I like the mummies and daddies
Clapping.

I like playing the bells
At school.
They sound like beautiful voices.

Jack Bowman (5)
Westways Primary School

Game Boy Vs School

In the morning
I play on my Game Boy.
I cover my ears to
Block out the dreadful sound
Nagging up the stairs.

'Tom come and get your shoes on!'

It is Mum.
I bellow,
'I'm coming!'

But really I don't
I just play on my Game Boy.

I snigger at the sound
Of my annoying sister's voice yelling,
'Tom, you're going to make me late, stupid!'
But I just ignore her
And play on my Game Boy.

It is now 20 to 9
But I don't care
I don't want to go to school today
As long as I've got my Game Boy, I'm okay.

Tom Bowman (7)
Westways Primary School

There Was A Young Girl Called Meg

There was a young girl called Meg
Whose favourite food was an egg
She bought so many
She spent every penny,
And oh how that girl had to beg.

Meg Plowright (9)
Westways Primary School

The Day My Teacher Got Struck By Lightning

One stormy winter's day, my teacher got struck by lightning,
Hooray!
Her hair looked like a fuzzy mushroom
She started running – *zoom.*

Mr Buzz called out, 'Behave!'
Joe kicked the ball, what a save!
She danced around with Mr Trotter
Always getting hotter and hotter.

Nothing could beat the fun of the day,
When my teacher got struck by *lightning!*

Hooray!
          Hooray!
   Hooray!

Sanaa Ghori (10)
Westways Primary School

My *Enormous* Guinea Pig

I have an *enormous* guinea pig,
That has a lot to eat.
He has a huge bowl,
And he's as fat as a cat.

His best friend's a rabbit,
That's almost as big as he is.
His mum is small,
And you should see his dad.

My mum thinks he's an *alien*,
All the way from outer space,
I just hope he has a long life,
So he can be there for you and me.

Joanna Lee (9)
Westways Primary School

Y6 Cool

Y6
Y5
Y4
Y3
Y6 are the coolest in the school, oh yeh they rule,
There's Hannah the spanner who fixes things with a mardy manner,
There's Fliss who likes to kiss in such bliss,
There's Rich who's a snitch who likes to play on the football pitch,
There's James who's a pain who likes to make up mad games,
There's Sarah the darer who likes to mess with Ciara,
There's Liam who likes to go to boring museums,
There's Joe who's slow and likes to play in the snow,
These are the people in the school,
Oh yeh they're cool but really I'm the best in the school.

Denver Baxter (11)
Westways Primary School

Have You Ever Seen?

Have you ever seen a kingfisher hiding and diving for food?
People looking for something to move?
When night begins the kingfisher zips,
With a flash of blue that will give you a fright!

Jessie Dooley (9)
Westways Primary School

Owl

It swoops down silently,
Hardly moving, only gliding
Its steel-like talons,
Just gripping, not slipping,
Its smooth feathers,
As smooth as light, as warm as fur,
It has the eyes of a telescope,
They scan the floor to find its prey,
Which is then eaten straight away,
No animal can escape from it,
It has the speed of a cheetah,
The strength of a bull
This beautiful creature lives in a tree
Not daring to come out when anyone can see.

Michael Wilsher (11)
Westways Primary School

Litter!

Litter here, litter there, litter
Everywhere I stare.

Under my feet, I wade over to my school.
In the hall I stare at the litter
That makes me bitter.

I go to the park, I see the fallen bins
Blown down in the heavy winds.

I play on the swings as I see
The fallen bins with all the litter
Blowing around on the ground.

People titter as I go and pick up the litter.

When I go home I tell my mum and dad
That this is really bad!

Sam Tadhunter (9)
Westways Primary School

Friends!

I thought I had lots of friends but it looks like that's coming to an end,
Because Jemma and Emma keep telling me lies
And Anna and Hannah keep tugging my ties.

Then there's Leone who never stops talking about her pony
And Claire who doesn't care about anything except for her hair.

I felt so sad without my friends all day that I decided to play with a
Lonely girl called May,
It didn't take long before we were having such fun,
What was the point of continuing to be glum?

The next day all six of my friends wanted to play
And they all said they were sorry for being mean yesterday.

A smile crossed my face
As my friends were now back in their rightful place.

Ceara Stones (11)
Westways Primary School

My Puppy

My puppy loves to bounce
My puppy loves to pounce
My puppy is mad!
My dad thinks my puppy is
Bad!

Beth Fairhurst (9)
Westways Primary School

My Rabbit

My rabbit is white,
And I think it's alright,
And I love him,
He eats up the sunflowers
He dances on the grass,
He chews up the weeds for us,
And I thank him at last,
My rabbit is white,
And I think it's alright
And I love him.

My rabbit is white,
But I think it's alright,
And I love him,
He chews up all the daffodils,
He prances on the grass,
When I get off the school bus,
I hug him at last,
My rabbit is white,
But I think it's alright,
And I love him.

Antonia Dore (9)
Westways Primary School

The Song Of Calmness

I was going cycling one day,
When I came along my way,
Along an old and bumpy track,
Away from the city, no looking back,
Soon the sounds of the forest filled my ears,
The calmness I'd been waiting for for years,
Then I heard that awful sound
It made my head spin round and round,
And together with that dreadful smell,
It made me want to scream and yell,
Then I saw at the end of the road,
A vehicle with man and load
There it was the motorbike,
Piercing the atmosphere like a spike,
He rode past without a care,
Smugness in his gleaming stare,
But we all knew what he had done,
He had tried to kill the calmness, but the
Calmness had won!

Claire Wilsher (9)
Westways Primary School